REVOLU-
TIONARY
THREADS

...U-
TIONARY
THREADS

RASTAFARI,
SOCIAL JUSTICE,
AND
COOPERATIVE
ECONOMICS

BOBBY
SULLIVAN

BROOKLYN, NEW YORK, USA
BALLYDEHOB, CO. CORK, IRELAND

Published by Akashic Books
©2018 Bobby Sullivan

ISBN: 978-1-61775-655-9
Library of Congress Control Number: 2018931235
First printing

Akashic Books
Brooklyn, New York, USA
Ballydehob, Co. Cork, Ireland
Twitter: @AkashicBooks
Facebook: AkashicBooks
E-mail: info@akashicbooks.com
Website: www.akashicbooks.com

We have sought to build the international unity of the spirit which today constitutes the most important force for good in the search for a lasting world peace and a decent way of life for humanity. With the raising of all men to their rightful dignity and honour as individuals, they will be able to regard their fellows, of whatever nation, of whatever race, of whatever religious, linguistic or historical tradition, as equals, without jealousy, without fear, without undue pride.

—Haile Selassie I

TABLE OF CONTENTS

DECOLONIZING OUR MINDS

This book is a collection of ideas I have gained through my experience as an activist and my participation with the Rastafari movement—I write for my sistren and brethren across the globe. I grew up making music in the punk scene in Washington, DC, which was centered around Dischord Records and the do-it-yourself (DIY) culture that continues to inspire many around the world. I have an international perspective because the city that raised me is a global hub. I have worked for food co-ops for most of my adult life, and this enables me to continue moving toward the goals I aspired to early on: promoting cultural tolerance and equitable relationships in an effort to simply get people to work, and to do it together for the benefit of all.

Each chapter of this book begins with the words to a song I have written, and these lyrics introduce the chapter's subject matter. I then describe the historical, cultural, and political significance behind the lyrics' meaning. In the ensuing pages, I will seek to expand upon alternative versions of history, citing diverse and colorful perspectives that are routinely neglected and marginalized in Western culture. In order to support my claims, I have cited as many sources as possible, so readers can follow the trail of authors frequently left out of historical records. In many ways, this is my own story too, because while this book is a collage of ideas, the subjects tie together quite nicely in my mind.

The movement of Rastafari is complex and largely misunderstood. There is tension with those trying to understand it, as well as within the movement itself, even regarding the teachings of its figurehead, Haile Selassie I—the emperor of Ethiopia from 1930 until a political coup in 1974. To further confound outsiders, the cultural context of Jamaica birthed this movement with a black nationalist perspective, yet the teachings of the emperor and some Rasta elders exhibit a more universal/humanist perspective. Because of this, the Rastafari movement is both inclusive and exclusive, and as history has played out, many diverse themes have predominated.

Although this book touches upon many themes, Rastafari is the glue that holds the work together. With that being said, I do not attempt to define Rastafari, as my perspective is derived chiefly from the movement's globalization rather than from my exposure to Jamaican elders. Of course, the Rastafari movement in the US has a different flavor than its Jamaican root; it is my belief that American Rastas should not try to emulate Jamaican culture, but instead take inspiration from the movement, especially from Haile Selassie I, and properly apply the sacred practices and teachings to one's own cultural context. In this book, I wish to give credit where credit is due. I want to honor the culture that ignited my journey. In a statement celebrating the work of Rahdakrishnan, Haile Selassie I offered some of his own key ambitions as a world leader: "To free the human race from superstition and fear that originate from ignorance; to enable him to transcend the apparent obstacles of race and religion; and to help him recognize the blood-ties of the whole human race."[1]

---

[1] Haile Selassie I, *Selected Speeches of His Imperial Majesty Haile Selassie I* (One Drop Books, 2000), p. 132–133.

Although Selassie I uses the word "him," he does not hold any lesser view of our sisters in the human family. As I will show you in this book, Haile Selassie I's teachings and the Rastafari movement cannot be reduced to patriarchal orders. "As with any spiritual order seeking perfection," notes Jake (John) Homiak, longtime Rastafari chronicler and director of the National Anthropological Archives at the Smithsonian Institution, "Rastafari is in a continual state of 'becoming' as individuals and mansions seek to refine their livity."

When I became exposed to diverse and global perspectives, the indoctrination I was raised with began to wither away, and I started to confront challenging realities about my native country. This book considers anticolonialism through the lens of an American grappling with the contradictions of an empire supposedly based on freedom. As an antidote to American hypocrisy, I will introduce the concept of cooperative economics. It is, I believe, *the way*: it is literally the intersection between democracy and the real economy, and it not so quietly builds a new world within our dying old one.

The Rastafari movement informs my critiques of capitalism. As Joseph Owens points out in his book *Dread*, Rastafari allows for a variety of perspectives:

> *Despite a certain value to perceiving the primordial Rasta doctrine before its syncretization with other ideas, the Rasta faith should also be appreciated for its ability to assimilate other doctrines which are in keeping with its own basic thrust. Indeed, much of the vitality and creativity of the Rastas stem from their openness to new ideas and progressive forces.*[2]

---

2 Joseph Owens, *Dread: The Rastafarians of Jamaica* (Heinemann, 1982), p. 24.

. . . Thus the Rastafarians sit and read with the news-paper in one hand, as it were, and the Bible in the other. They search out the manifold correlations between contemporary events and the sacred recorded history. Where correlations are found, they are used to help interpret the precise meaning of the present reality and to divine the course of future events.[3]

With this kind of holistic approach as context, this book plunges into American history, as well as the history of Rastafari, in order to demonstrate why Rastafari offers a suitable cure for contemporary ills. I also explore the American continent before European conquest, shed light on the first European settlements, pause briefly at the Civil War, and jump ahead to the revolutionary movements of the 1960s and '70s.

After surveying these histories, I examine another disturbing reality: through the hands of multinational corporations, fascism stands as the true victor of World War II, and it is alive and well in the US. Fascism has, in fact, morphed into a global force that works to colonize people who lack the means to coexist as partners in the "empire of money," which is a term the Zapatistas of Mexcio coined for such international aggression.[4]

Even after my extensive research, I've concluded that human history is truly a mystery. So much persists by word of mouth, and then gets recorded long after actual events took place. No standardized history book, or any singular source, can possibly deliver our whole incredible story. Therefore, many perspectives need to be considered. Too often, con-

---

3   *Ibid*, p. 37.

4   El Kilombo Intergaláctico, *Beyond Resistance: Everything. An Interview with Subcomandante Insurgente Marcos* (PaperBoat Press, 2008), p. 4.

querors and power brokers write their own versions of history. This volume hopes to explore different perspectives and introduce narratives and ideas unlikely to be told in conventional historical renderings.

After all, American history is rife with so-called culture bandits, as author Del Jones labeled Elvis Presley. This means that many people, including some rock and rollers, appropriate and repurpose culture that is not their own, profit from it, and ignore the complexities and legacies of colonial history. This cultural highjacking has happened to and even within Rastafari, largely due to the fact that it is decentralized and highly pluralistic. As Jake Homiak posited in *When Goldilocks Met the Dreadlocks: Reflections on the Contributions of Carole D. Yawney to Rastafari Studies*: "Even in Jamaica during the early 1970s, Rastafari had become too organizationally complex and ideologically dynamic for any one researcher, or even any single Rastafari participant, to grasp in its fullness."

Due to my own personal journey, I see the world of Rastafari as a living culture that transforms perceptions in cosmic proportions. Rastafari is mystical and mysterious, challenging and serious. It is unlikely that one can truly "overstand" Rastafari from an outside perspective.

> *"Why yuh talk 'bout research? Research! No, is an I-search,"* Bongo Watto said in 1983. *"The mon haffi search himself first. An' yuh cyan study Rastafari. Mi say, no mon can study Rastafari. Yuh can only live Rastafari!"*[5]

---

5   John Homiak, "When Goldilocks Met the Dreadlocks: Reflections on the Contributions of Carole D. Yawney to Rastafari Studies," *Let Us Start With Africa: Foundations of Rastafari Scholarship*, edited by Jahlani Niaah and Erin MacLeod (University of the West Indies Press, 2013), p. 61.

As our modern minds work to untangle the past, we can uncover different modes of thinking that dominated ancient times, before Greek and Roman historical, philosophical, and spiritual perspectives took over. Yet Rastafari's culture of "livity," with its dual modes of cognition—reasoning and meditation—can help us reach beyond the current smoke-screen to appreciate ancient thinking in a new way.

Beginning in 476 CE, the Romans and the Dark Ages cast a Eurocentric shadow over world history. Even though the Greeks looked to Africa as the birthplace of their spirituality and sciences, the Romans severed the link to this glorious past. The rest of Europe followed suit, thus many significant ideas, philosophies, and religions were effectively erased from dominant consciousness. Throughout time, pluralism is stamped out again and again, replaced by new forms of fundamentalism.

For example, many students of history don't know that Islamic Spain was a religiously tolerant empire from 750 CE up to the mid-1400s, and essentially spawned the Renaissance in Europe. What is now known as Kabbalah in the Hebraic tradition, and Sufism in the Islamic tradition, sprang from Islamic Spain, as did paper, sewers, streetlights, and many of the sciences with which Europe was just becoming acquainted. The Crusades not only appropriated these technologies, they destroyed the lives, wealth, and land of the people who pioneered them, along the way eliminating the notion of religious tolerance.

It is my contention that we are presently living out the legacies of European colonialism and conquest, changing our relationships with language, religion, and culture. The colonial intrusion and its economic structures have persisted and gone increasingly global. Those of us caught up in the web of

these controlling tendencies need to take action, both physical and spiritual. Ultimately, we must decolonize our very
minds.

Haile Selassie I's message continues to be compelling for
those questioning colonial powers. Anyone searching for new
meaning in their life will find Rasta principals useful in dis-
mantling poisonous concepts that compartmentalize human
beings. Many people, myself included, don't fit neatly within
the confines of colonialist definitions of race and culture. In
this context, Haile Selassie I's words are especially poignant:

> We must become something we have never been and for
> which our education and experience and environment
> have ill prepared us. We must become bigger than we
> have been, more courageous, greater in spirit, larger in
> outlook. We must become members of a new race, over-
> coming petty prejudice, owing our ultimate allegiance not
> to nations but to our fellow men within the human
> community.[6]

The time is here: more people must connect with a rightful path, even if cautiously. The sacred "I" is our primal connection, which also suggests our differentiation from others.
No matter how hard people try to group themselves into
races, cultures, nationalities, social groups, or even genders,
every single life-form on earth is undeniably unique. Nature
proves over and over again that such diversity is a strength.

The concept of "I" is central in Rastafari spirituality, and
many words are reconstructed to reflect this. For example,
"heights" becomes "Ites," "brethren" and "sistren" become

---

6   Haile Selassie I, *Selected Speeches of His Imperial Majesty Haile Selassie I* (One Drop
Books, 2000), pgs. 377–378.

"Idren," "unity" becomes "Inity," and many more I-words are created on the spot. "I" also replaces "you" or "me," which in turn denotes our equal footing. Most importantly, "I and I" is often used to refer to oneself or another individual to reflect divinity in the form of a oneness between the Most High, Jah, and every person.

Many forces on earth elude our understanding, and we tend to fix ideas into our psyche that may not be healthy for us or those around us. As humans, we are all creators of vibration and intent, able to bring forth great beauty and harm in a single breath. Therefore, our relationship with our life force in all its modalities needs to be constantly examined. Thoughts, through words, physically manifest—we are agents of action, powered by impulse, shaping our shared reality. As Haile Selassie I stated: "It is only when a people strike an even balance between scientific progress and spiritual and moral advancement that it can be said to possess a wholly perfect and complete personality and not a lopsided one."[7]

PUNKY REGGAE PARTY

I grew up a racially ambiguous white kid in Washington, DC, a city with a large African American majority at that time. No matter which racial group I tried to fit into, I was invariably painted as "other." This led to a preoccupation with race issues at an early age. I was certainly drawn to rebellion, so it was an inconvenient truth for me that my father worked for the CIA. This led me to acquire role models outside my home, who raised me with specific cultural tendencies and tastes. In DC, most of the teachers, administrators, local pol-

---

7 *Ibid*, p. 664.

iticians, and other authority figures were African Americans, as were many artists and musicians, such as Bad Brains, a Rasta punk band I deeply admired.

Bad Brains were an important synchronization of differing cultural tastes. They gave many kids an outlet that we had only experienced before with British punk bands, like those mentioned in Bob Marley's song "Punky Reggae Party": the Jam, the Damned, the Clash. Like us American kids, the British musicians grew up with West Indian influences. This multicultural expression was similarly exemplified in 2 Tone Records' ska upsurge, not to mention the Rock Against Racism concerts that took place in England and Washington, DC, in the seventies and eighties.

Bad Brains were devout Rastas. Although bands like the Clash paid tribute to Rastafari, the Bad Brains were a spiritual force, not just activists. And although reggae is a perfect platform for the platitudes of Rastafari, the intensity of the Bad Brains' blistering time signatures let their messages come through in awe-inspiring ways.

The 1980s American punk music scene was not a star-studded affair. Although certain punk musicians certainly had the charisma to become stars, the public was not yet ready for their chaotic new genre. This meant that most punk bands at the time were very approachable and down-to-earth.

In this vein, Bad Brains singer H.R. approached me one day in the mid-eighties and invited my band to play with them at a small club in downtown DC. Afterward, he invited me to hang out at his place. This is where my journey with Rastafari began. As a seventeen-year-old, I gained an older brother who I could look to for spiritual and practical guidance. (My older blood brother Mark and Ian MacKaye, who still runs Dischord Records, were also important role models for me.) H.R. and the Bad Brains exemplified to me how Rastafari could be embodied in America in an honest way.

Around the same time, my high school friend and bandmate Johnny Temple and I ventured out to see Toots and the Maytals perform; they were one of the Jamaican reggae bands that Bob Marley mentioned in "Punky Reggae Party." Johnny and I were too young to get into the show, but he had the brilliant idea of sneaking into the club through the back door by paying a roadie. It worked.

After the show, Johnny and I ventured outside to the back door of the club to see if we could meet the band. We started talking to an older couple also waiting there. After a brief silence, they asked us how we got into reggae. We told them that we often listened to *Night of the Living Dread,* a radio show on WHFS hosted by Doctor Dread, a local DJ. The man replied, "I'm Doctor Dread."[8]

After a brief conversation, he suggested we come by his record store in nearby Kensington, Maryland. Soon thereafter, Johnny and I made our initial trek to RAS Records, Doctor Dread's reggae record label and distribution company. When we arrived, singer Peter Broggs was at the office; RAS had recently put out his new album, *Rastafari Liveth!*, which was the label's first release. After some encouragement, Johnny and I bought Peter's record. He was more than happy to sign both of our copies.

RAS became a regular outing for Johnny and me, and we both eventually got jobs there. We started meeting artists like Michigan & Smiley, Augustus Pablo, and Ini Kamoze, to name just a few. The people at RAS introduced me to dub

---

8 For a fascinating look at this man, see *The Half That's Never Been Told* by Doctor Dread (Akashic Books, 2015).

poet Mutabaruka, and gave me books like *Itations of Jamaica and I Rastafari* by Millard Faristzaddi and Joseph Owens's *Dread: The Rastafarians of Jamaica.*

Itations was what first revealed to me the many shades of Rastafari. As an American with budding dreadlocks, it was encouraging to know I was not alone in embracing a culture adopted by many people around the world. Alternatively, Owens's book, juxtaposed with Horace Campbell's *Rasta and Resistance*, further informed my Rastafari education. The former was written by an American clergyman and focused on the spiritual nature of Rastafari, while the latter dissected the revolutionary nature of the movement and how it related to Pan-Africanism.

At RAS Records, Johnny and I were in charge of shipping and receiving, which meant we were opening and responding to letters from reggae fans around the world—this included inmates from various US prisons. We engaged in extended correspondence with many of these prisoners. As we continued to learn about their financial hardships, we sent them albums from our own collections, since they were invariably financially strapped.

My early connection with inmates was an important precursor to my work several decades later with the Rastafari UniverSoul Fellowship Prison Ministry, which eventually led to a meeting with Haile Selassie I's grandson, Prince Ermias Sahle Selassie, and a trip to the UN headquarters in New York City with a delegation of Rasta representatives. Still later, my work with food cooperatives brought me to Jamaica, where I was able to connect with Rastafari Ancients and a Maroon community, and learn more about the harsh realities of global trade. I traveled to Havana a few months after that to work with Cuban co-ops.

Throughout the world, people have so much in common, yet there are many painful truths in history we must continue to grapple with. I hope these pages help you find your own way so you can better know the I (that is you), and truly learn to love and appreciate the I's that are invariably painted as others.

CHAPTER 1

PILTDOWN MAN

*How can I be aware? Truth in history is unfortunately
rare,*
*So many stories abound everywhere—which conspiracy
do I let become a part of me?*
*You can take a course at the university, they can tell you
all about ancient Greece,*
*But do they go back to tell you the story of the ancient
ones in Kemet who started history?*

It's like the Piltdown Man . . .

*Have you ever heard about Cahokia, an East St. Louis
ancient pyramid not spoken of?*
*You thought you knew the history of America, so what
of the South American temples that predate the Bering
Strait?*
*Did they really tell you about Akhenaten, his religion,
and the young Tutankhamun?*
Did they tell you what we all have in common?
Did they tell you we all came from ancient Africa?

It's like the Piltdown Man who satisfied their story,
They wanted to believe so they could have some glory.
The Piltdown Man—human fossils in Eurasia.
If you believe in Columbus this one won't phase you.
The Piltdown Man—did the research skimp?
Were the accepted bones orangutan or chimp?
The Piltdown Man—the history makers,
They throw out a story and most men are takers.
Most men are followers.

Did they ever tell you about King Selassie? He slew the
  dragon without a lethal posse.
On King Selassie we have to break the silence, expelled
  the enemy without spreading violence,
So to the King we give thanks and praises, and to Em-
  press Menen, she's the balance of the ages.
Opened the book, they loosed the Seven Seals,
Set the example, so Truth could be revealed.

It's like the ancient books—the Romans burned collections,
Then they made their own without any election.
The ancient books—some made it to the Bible,
Then came the Dead Sea Scrolls, now their version's
  deniable.

It's like the Piltdown Man . . .

The Piltdown Man controversy is an excellent metaphor for history as we know it, involving an alleged
discovery of early human bones at the Piltdown vil-
lage in East Sussex, England, in 1912. Charles Dawson and
other archeologists claimed their findings confirmed the
connection between ape and man. Teaching human evolution was against the law in state-funded schools in the early
twentieth century, so the Piltdown Man was used by the defense in the 1925 Scopes "Monkey" trial to prove evolution's
scientific validation.

Forty years after the initial discovery, *Time* magazine
published scientific evidence debunking the Piltdown Man
findings as a hoax. The bones were an orangutan's jawbone
combined with a human skull. Originally the find was presented as a missing link between apes and humans, but
Creationists used the hoax as an example of dishonest pa-
leontologists, which fueled the public's suspicion of science.

Significantly, the Piltdown Man case exposed Western desperation to portray England as the cradle of humanity instead of Africa. A report on PBS recounts how the scandal's announcement in the *New York Times* created a ripple effect: "Several highly respected and serious scientists were deceived and their reputations forever tarnished, and years of research and thought had been wasted on trying to analyze and fit the fake fossils into the record of human evolution."[9] Even today, as cultural biases and manufactured facts are pumped through media sources all around us, accessing truth remains difficult.

JOHN'S REVELATION, AFRICA'S REDEMPTION, AND THE HAZE OF HUMAN HISTORY

The Piltdown discovery, and the ensuing intent to elevate the European link to evolutionary dominance, carried with it implications for non-Western ideologies. Aware of historical and scientific malpractice, Rastafari people provide a more technical convergence of African and biblical history. Throughout the Bible, they point out, Africa is a significant spiritual and historical hub. Revelation 5:5 states: "And one of the elders saith unto me, Weep not: behold, the Lion of the tribe of Judah, the Root of David, hath prevailed to open the book, and to loose the seven seals thereof." Haile Selassie I's lineage can be traced back to David through Solomon and Makeda, the Queen of Sheba. It was their union which gave birth to the Ethiopian king who would keep the Ark of the Covenant and the traditions intact, when Israel fell apart and the Holy Temple was destroyed by Nebuchadnezzar.

Haile Selassie I worked hard to open the door to a deeper

---

9 "People and Discoveries: Piltdown Man Is Revealed as Fake," PBS, 1953.

relationship with the Bible and broader perspectives of its historical roots. The Rastafari movement, it appears, provided a missing link to John's Revelation in the New Testament. Rastafari people are crucial to this prophecy, bringing the reality of the Bible into our present era, countering the "one mind" of the fascists and aligning history with the "Lamb."

> *These have one mind, and shall give their power and strength unto the beast.*
> *These shall make war with the Lamb, and the Lamb shall overcome them: for he is the Lord of lords and King of kings; and they that are with him are called, and chosen, and faithful.*
> —Revelation 17:13–14

> *And he hath on his vesture and on his thigh a name written, KING OF KINGS, AND LORD OF LORDS.*
> —Revelation 19:16

Dating back centuries, "King of Kings, Lord of Lords, Conquering Lion of the Tribe of Judah" was a traditional title for Ethiopian emperors. Fascism gained prominence during Haile Selassie I's leadership, and conjointly many Rastafari sistren and brethren consider him as Christ, "the Lamb" in his kingly character—the second and last advent.

The king of Ethiopia's deified significance is recorded in the New Testament. In the book of Revelation, a nation is redeemed to God (Elohim) by the Lion of the Tribe of Judah, and a multinational people were to become kings and priests, redeemed by this figure.[10] Haile Selassie I, who held the title

---

10 Revelation 5:9–10

"Lion of the Tribe of Judah" from 1930 through the 1970s, was the last king of the very first nation on earth. Many Christians are not aware that Haile Selassie I was considered by the church to be the "Elect of God" and Africa's "Defender of the [Christian] Faith." Axum, Ethiopia's capital in the first century CE, officially adopted Christianity in the early fourth century, just before Rome did.[11] Some say the new religion had taken hold in Ethiopia even earlier. In any event, the region had already been steeped in Old Testament teachings for centuries.

The Bible needs to be approached with an historical perspective to be truly understood. Without knowledge of the roots of the names, places, and histories, we are left to accept dominant schools of thought that have theologically shackled the Western world; conventional biblical misinterpretations have harmed humanity for centuries. For instance, when one considers the teachings ascribed to Jesus Christ, it is disturbing to discover that the first slave ship carrying human cargo in chains to the Americas was called the *Good Ship Jesus*.

The Old Testament, the book that is the primary scriptural source for Judaism, Christianity, and Islam, is approached openly by Rastas. Rastafari brings a unifying perspective to the echoes of humanity's original culture and faith, where reasoning has a place and so does debate, balanced by meditation and contemplation. In the conflicting realms of our diverse religious teachings, Haile Selassie I is clear: "As we guarantee to each the right to worship as he chooses, so we denounce the policy that sets man against man on the issue of religion."[12]

---

11 David Robinson, *Muslim Societies in African History* (Cambridge University Press, 2004), p. 109, and Richard Pankhurst, *The Ethiopians: A History* (Wiley-Blackwell, 1998), p. 24

12 Teferra Haile-Selassie, *The Ethiopian Revolution 1974–1991: From a Monarchical Autocracy to a Military Oligarchy* (Routledge, 1997), p. 71

RASTAFARI: A COLLECTIVE CONSCIOUSNESS

Growing up in Washington, DC, I met many Jamaican immigrants and Rastas from across the world. Their fresh and diverse perspectives regarding ancient history and current events conveyed an openness to our shared humanity, despite our varied cultures. Gerald Hausman echoes this dynamic in his epic edition of the *Kebra Negast:*

> *There are as many kinds of Rastas as the reeds that grow on the riverbank. There's baldhead Rasta, like me. There's white Rasta, like you. There's rootical Rasta—you know what I mean? Just rootsy people, who keep the faith, but don't believe in any ceremony, or chant, or Bible business. There's Congo Dread and Coptic Dread. But all stem from the same thing, and it all go through the same place, the heart, you know.*[13]

This Rastafari movement was greatly influenced by well-known prophets like Marcus Garvey and Leonard Howell, but it was also later influenced by the American Civil Rights Movement, the Black Power movement, and various international anticolonial movements. Elders in Jamaica had shined a light so bright that Rastafari had become its own global movement, with universalizing tendencies.

Rastafari's teachings have an international appeal, so as elders continue to protect the roots, the tree continues to form many branches, so to speak. Jake Homiak defers to fellow scholar Carole Yawney in order to describe the difficulties in defining the movement as just one thing:

---

13 Gerald Hausman, *The Kebra Nagast: The Lost Bible of Rastafarian Wisdom and Faith from Ethiopia and Jamaica* (St. Martin's Press, 1997), pgs. 156–157.

She was clear that Rastafari, as a large-scale, dynamic and heterogeneous movement, encapsulated multiple frames of reference that could at times be potentially contradictory (for example, black supremacy versus planetary humanism) and that certain themes—both by researchers and participants—might be variously "centered" or "de-centered," elevated or subordinated at any given period or point in time. She understood as well that the discursive space that she occupied as an ethnographer with the Rastafari was not one of shared circumstances in which all were seen as having equal freedom and opportunity to speak or represent their particular orientation at any given point in time. Recognition of this diversity— this asserted "unity without uniformity"—was one of the reasons that Carole insisted that a researcher should generalize about the movement only with extreme caution.[14]

Because Ethiopia was the birthplace of humanity and the source of the Nile, Rastafari looks to the country as a Holy Land. Ancient Ethiopian culture fed the Pharaohs of Egypt, who in turn gave instruction to the Greeks. Ethiopia was the first Christian nation and remained so after Roman conquests. Ethiopians then helped nurture the birth and early rise of Islam, promoting a peaceful coexistence with Christianity by acknowledging the similarities between the two religions.

Haile Selassie I was a champion of religious tolerance, protecting Ethiopia against colonialism and fascism. Al-

---

14 John Homiak, "When Goldilocks Met the Dreadlocks: Reflections on the Contributions of Carole D. Yawney to Rastafari Studies," *Let Us Start With Africa: Foundations of Rastafari Scholarship,* edited by Jahlani Niaah and Erin MacLeod (University of the West Indies Press, 2013), pgs. 85–86.

though he was unapologetic when it came to militant self-defense, his governing approach was primarily diplomatic, even when confronted with brutal violence. He was "an active champion of African independence, African unity, and Africa's modern development. He often defended the rights of the poor and suffering nations of the world, firstly at the League of Nations and later at the United Nations."[15]

At the end of the nineteenth century, Ethiopia was the only country in Africa to maintain its independence from European colonization. Decades later, however, Ethiopia fell to the Italian fascist aggressors in the lead-up to World War II. The Italians were later expelled, and Haile Selassie I returned to power in 1941, reigning until he was overthrown by a Communist coup in 1974.

This complex history begs the question: when did Rastafari form? Some say it began with human history itself, recorded in hieroglyphics on Egyptian pyramids. Many priests and dignitaries in those ancient times wore dreadlocks, as shown in characterizations within the temples and in the papyri they produced. The ancient Egyptian *Book of Coming Forth by Day*, the so-called *Egyptian Book of the Dead*, calls Asar (Osiris) "King of Kings and Lord of Lords," the same title Ethiopian emperors assumed. The book also proclaims, "The Great Council is in Rastau!" Rastafari spiritual precepts and practices have been handed down throughout time, even from the most remote periods of our history.[16]

It is important to note why the movement is called *Rastafari* instead of *Selassie I*. Lij Tafari was pronounced "Ras"

---

15   Ras Sekou S. Tafari in the introduction to *The Wise Mind of H.I.M. Emperor Haile Selassie* by H.I.H. Prince Ermias Sahle Selassie (Frontline Books, 2004), p. 15.

16   Aakhun George W. Singleton, *Esoteric Atannuology, Egyptology and Rastafariology, Volume I* (Enlightenment Publications, 1997).

and Regent by Empress Zewditu I in the early 1900s. Tafari's father served under Emperor Menelik II, fighting by his side when they expelled the Italians from Ethiopia in the Battle of Adwa in 1896 (a scene depicted in the gatefold of Bob Marley's album *Confrontation*). Zewditu I reigned over Ethiopia from 1916 to 1930, and Ras Tafari publicly became Haile Selassie I when he and Empress Menen I ascended the throne in 1930. Thus, the movement takes its name from Selassie I's birth name and the title he had when the news first appeared in a Jamaican newspaper.

Rasta elders were able to bring forth powerful truths, which at once seemed long forgotten. Through the Nyahbinghi Order, phrases such as "Word, Sound is Power" and "I and I," as well as concepts like "Ital" harkened back to the ancient order of Melchizedek's mystic consciousness and other mysteries of ancient African spirituality in a crucial way. This caught the attention of many religious scholars and educators.

The Rastafari movement foundationally stems from several strains of thought in Jamaica, wherein Rastafari participants are organized into "houses" or "mansions," as in John 14:2: "In my Father's house are many mansions." The early mansions included the Nyahbinghi, Bobo Ashanti, Twelve Tribes of Israel, and adherents of the Ethiopian Orthodox Tawahedo Church. Here's McPherson's perspective on the early Rastafari powers:

> *All four major early Rasta Precursors/Communes and Organizations represented the continued Internationalist Pan-Africanist/Ethiopianist stream. This was a Tradition of a continuing "Ethiopianism" (the Independent Church Movement—breakaway from European domination). It*

is, however, the "integration" of these diversified Black
Churches: "Cults"/Organizations: Social Movements,
that has given birth to the Rastafari Faith—as a Church/
Universal Church/Religion.

The Inspirational Creativity of All these Founding
Fathers have to be accredited for the spread of the Ras-
tafari Movement. They moved from an individualistic
level of religious emanation to a "collective representa-
tive" level.[17]

Early Rastafari elders preached Rasta as a way of life
rather than a religion. But as McPherson points out, Rastafari did ultimately become a religion. With its close biblical
relation, some scholars, priests, and even Rastas have tried
to fit Rastafari into a Christian paradigm, but have ultimately
found that it cannot be experienced through such a narrow
prism. Instead, the multitude of mind-sets within Rastafari
can act as a healing balm between adherents of Judaism,
Christianity, and Islam.

Still, Rastafari is viewed by much of the modern world
as a niche movement with temporal symbols and sacraments
popularized and obscured by reggae music and consumer culture. Many casual reggae fans are not aware how political,
spiritual, and informative the music is, and how deeply it is
rooted in Rastafari culture. Again, McPherson offers an interesting perspective regarding Rastafari's complexities:

Rastafari—as such is a Social Cosmology, theological
ideology, ideology of development and a ongoing process
of the re-contextualization of history, that represents a

---

17   *Ibid*, p. 26.

Emancipatory path for ALL "DOWNPRESSED" (op-pressed) Peoples of the Earth, from the political and spiritual Caesars of this World.

Rastafari is a created tactical cultural—ideological People's Front, poised to effect that identity change/acceptance of Our cultural identity, and effectuate that necessary politics of liberation, that so many "religions" and Black Churches have not yet come to grips with.[18]

McPherson considers the early development of Rastafari in Jamaica as a continuation of the Pan-Africanists' Ethiopianism. On the subject of Pan-Africanism in the Americas and the Caribbean, Haile Selassie I stated the following during a 1973 celebration of the Organization of African Unity:

Finally, as we look back on the past . . . and look forward to many year(s) to come, it would afford us a longer historical perspective to remember that the search for unity among peoples of Africa has its roots in Pan-Africanism. Pan-Africanism grew out of the efforts of African nationals and descendants of Africans in the new world who sought to establish collective strength by affirming the validity of their cultures and civilization. This movement gradually became an indispensable part of the struggle for independence and freedom.[19]

This is a huge nod to all the Pan-Africanists throughout the diaspora who worked so hard to forge their own path through the difficulties they faced confronting the colonial and neocolonial powers. This crisscrossing of cultures back

---

18 *Ibid*, p. 46.

19 *Ibid*, p. i.

and forth between the "new world" and Africa created fertile soil for the birth of a new movement with global implications. "Undoubtedly, [early Rasta leaders like] Nathaniel Hibbert and Leonard Howell would have heard of King Ja Ja of Opobo, the African king from West Africa who was deported to the Caribbean in 1887," wrote Horace Campbell in *Rasta and Resistance*.[20] King Jaja was a "famous entrepreneur who was exiled to the island of St. Vincent in the Lesser Antilles by the British," according to Homiak. This was "for his refusal to cease levying taxes on British merchants who participated in the extensive palm oil trade that he controlled. The British, of course, did this kind of thing everywhere and destroyed local control of indigenous resources."

Much has also been written about Rastafari's early West African and Hindu influences, especially by way of Leonard Howell and his incredibly pivotal Pinnacle commune in Jamaica.[21] Howell is credited as the first person to successfully connote the significance between Haile Selassie I's coronation and divinity.

ARISE YE MIGHTY PEOPLE

In the 1990s, Terisa E. Turner published the book *Arise Ye Mighty People!*, which largely draws its premise from the legendary Caribbean thinker C.L.R. James. James was a prominent and influential Trinidadian Socialist historian who authored many books, pamphlets, speeches, and essays, and was considered an influential voice in postcolonial literature and "a pioneer of Autonomist Marxism."[22] Turner explains:

---

20 Horace Campbell, *Rasta and Resistance: From Marcus Garvey to Walter Rodney* (Africa World Press, 1987), p. 102.

21 See Rex Nettleford, "Hindu Influences on Rastafarianism," in *Caribbean Quarterly Monograph* (University of the West Indies Press, 1985).

22 Gary Kinsman, "The Politics of Revolution: Learning from Autonomist Marxism,"

"A decade before Bob Marley made reggae a powerful weapon for revolution, James pointed to the future in the present. He saw that the rejection of capitalist mainstream relations by Black Muslims, Rastafari, Africa's Mau Mau, and white proto hippies or beatniks constituted a global watershed from which would emerge a new global society."[23] Turner further suggests that James "emphasized that the importance of Rastafari was not only their rejection of official society but their creation of a new one."[24]

Turner pulls together diverse perspectives from multiple authors in order to give voice to a rejuvenated form of Rastafari: "Emerging from the contradictions of post-WWII capitalism . . . a black feminist movement has grown up to shape a 'new Rastafari.'" She continues to propose the three "crises of capitalism"—the early twentieth century, the 1930s through the 1960s, and the more current period of structural adjustment programs. "Using the concept of the 'male deal' to examine dynamics during each crisis," Turner argues, "the 'new Rastafari' is part of a broad egalitarian social movement of resistance to structural adjustment and affirmation of communal control over resources."[25]

Following the footsteps of Walter Rodney, a professor at the University of the West Indies in the 1960s, Turner consults C.L.R. James's work and begins a sober analysis of more recent events in African society. Along with the aforementioned author Carole Yawney's assistance, Turner sheds light on the history of Nyahbinghi, a feminine force from East

---

El Kilombo.

23 Terisa E. Turner with Bryan J. Ferguson, *Arise Ye Mighty People!: Gender, Class and Race in Popular Struggles* (Africa World Press, 1994), p. 13.

24 *Ibid*, p. 11.

25 *Ibid*, p. 9.

Africa that successfully resisted European colonialism. Rastafari culture is seen as a common thread for those engaged in a struggle against globalization. In regards to this theory, Turner writes:

> Rasta mystical art "welcomes evocative imagery from other traditions," and reflects struggles of all people. The range of symbolic ambiguities "encourages oppressed people everywhere to articulate and resolve their grievances with redemptive imagery." The result is consensus which is part of the groundwork for moving toward power to use in regaining an "Eden" where all things are possible . . . a core theme in Rastafari: the sistren and brethren are exiles from Eden, from Africa, cast out by slavery into the diaspora. This chapter argues that the globalization of Rastafari is fundamentally due to the promise it contains to all of us who experience exile or alienation.[26]

As Rastafari consciousness continues to spread across the world, the movement builds upon itself and transforms existing norms. Some indigenous cultures, including Native Americans, are embracing the tenets of Rastafari in order to liberate themselves from crony Western capitalism, and in the age of the Internet, the movement's international allure is increasing. As Haile Selassie I said, "To start anything is simple; to develop it and bring it to a successful culmination takes great effort."[27] Jamaicans propelled Rastafari into a global phenomenon, and now Rastafari exists in a trans-

---

26 *Ibid*, p. 75.

27 Haile Selassie I, *Important Utterances of H.I.M. Emperor Haile Selassie I* (One Drop Books, 2000), p. 20.

local digital space that allows people from all different races, nationalities, and cultures to embrace faith and reason with one another. Still, the importance of the personal touch one gets from communicating face-to-face cannot be diminished.

I can recall many times when Rastafari reasoning sessions induced revelations and realizations at a food co-op just outside of DC called Glut. One time I was reasoning with a brother from Eritrea, who I had met at a recent demonstration in Philadelphia for Mumia Abu-Jamal. I was curious to hear this brother's perspective on Rastafari because I had recently learned about Eritrean hardship as a result of several of Haile Selassie I's policies put forth in an effort to bring Eritrea back into the Ethiopian nation. The Italians used Eritrea as a base the two times they invaded Ethiopia. Eritrea eventually became an independent state, cutting off Ethiopia from the Red Sea and effectively landlocking it in the north. When I asked the young Eritrean if he believed Haile Selassie I to be God, he replied that although he was a Rasta, he did not believe in Haile Selassie I's divinity; he had heard too many negative things about the emperor from older relatives.

We were in the middle of a small grocery store and many people around us were shopping. An older Rasta, who had overheard the Eritrean and me talking, quickly stepped in. He interjected by reciting Isaiah 5:26: "And he will lift up an ensign to the nations from far, and will hiss unto them from the end of the earth: and, behold, they shall come with speed swiftly." The old Rasta then determinedly said that because Haile Selassie I had ruled as an African man, it would be hard for those on the continent to recognize his human form as divine. It would be the "nations from far" who would bring that consciousness home. As pointed out earlier, Haile Selassie I himself said that the Pan-Africanism which sprouted up in the diaspora influenced that same movement in Africa.

After my encounter with this older Rasta, I dug deeper into the Bible. Here are two poignant passages in *Isaiah* that resonated with me:

And he shall set up an ensign for the nations, and shall assemble the outcasts of Israel, and gather the dispersed of Judah from the four corners of the earth.
—Isaiah 11:12

For I am the Lord thy God, the Holy One of Israel, thy Saviour: I gave Egypt for thy ransom, Ethiopia and Seba for thee.

Since thou wast precious in my sight, thou hast been honourable, and I have loved thee: therefore will I give men for thee, and people for thy life.

Fear not: for I am with thee: I will bring thy seed from the east, and gather thee from the west;

I will say to the north, Give up; and to the south, Keep not back: bring my sons from far, and my daughters from the ends of the earth;

Even every one that is called by my name: for I have created him for my glory, I have formed him; yea, I have made him.

Bring forth the blind people that have eyes, and the deaf that have ears.

Let all the nations be gathered together, and let the people be assembled: who among them can declare this, and shew us former things? Let them bring forth their witnesses, that they may be justified: or let them hear, and say, It is truth.
—Isaiah 43:3-9

As Rastas, we consider Africa's historical and modern bondage to be the source of most human suffering. Africa was the root of every Abrahamic religion; Africa was the beginning of us all. Reconnecting to Africa—the birthplace of humanity—seems like the most obvious method to heal history's wounds, not as nations, but as family, focusing on similarities and tolerating differences. Continental Africa provides a wealth of possibility for humans to overstand our shared history. Synthesizing Africa's inscrutable role in human development, Drusilla D. Houston offers the following in her book *Wonderful Ethiopians of the Ancient Cushite Empire*:

> *Astronomical observations, arithmetic, geometry, architecture, all the arts, and nearly all the sciences, and industries of the present day, were known [in Egypt] when the Greeks were still cave men. The origin of the sciences and many moral precepts, still taught from the wisdom of the ancients, were recorded upon the Egyptian papyri or on the monuments. The very groove of our present thought had its origin upon the banks of the Nile.*[28]

Language, religion, science, agriculture, animal domesticity, and foods such as wheat, barley, oats, rye, cotton, millet, bananas, and coffee, all came from Africa.[29] Stephen of Byzantium identified Ethiopia as "the first established country on earth; and the people were the first, who introduced the worship of the Gods and who enacted laws."[30]

28 Drusilla Dunjee Houston, *Wonderful Ethiopians of the Ancient Cushite Empire* (Peggy Bertram Publishing, 2007), pgs. 57–58.

29 John G. Jackson, *Ages of Gold and Silver and Other Short Sketches of Human History* (American Atheist Press, 1990), p. 30.

30 J.A. Rogers, *Nature Knows No Color-Line* (Helga M. Rogers, 1952), p. 32.

WHAT IS NATURAL?

Part of Rastafari's primary appeal to me as a young person was exploring how Rastafari people interacted with the natural world. As Joseph Owens explained, "The Rastaman here in the West is striving to return to the natural state of affairs represented symbolically and actually by Africa."[31] In my teens, I was interested in learning more about African culture. If the Piltdown discovery disrupted the collective thinking about how early humans interrelated with their environment, Rastafari was revealing a truly symbiotic relationship with nature, before the Europeans started to dominate. Further detailing Rastafari's interdependence with nature, Joseph Owens stated:

> In professing to be people devoted to nature and the good earth, the Rastafarians reject the western civilization which has divorced itself from the true sources of life for too long and has worshipped instead all types of artificiality. Nature is a basic concept in the Rastafarian creed, one that helps to explain other key doctrines, such as repatriation, the use of ganja, the growing of locks and beards, the humanity of God, and the "churchly" nature of the human body, to name a few.[32]

What we consider to be "natural" determines how we relate to the physical world—our families, bodies, and concepts of time all hinge upon the natural world. The quality in which we interact with such physical and spiritual realms, however, is directly impacted by how deeply we reason and

31 Joseph Owens, *Dread: The Rastafarians of Jamaica* (Heinemann, 1982), p. 148.

32 *Ibid*, pgs. 147–148.

consider our existences. But these days, we tend to lean toward life's blind conveniences, losing our better instincts within screen and substances; most of our intelligence resides in the computers we now employ. Our collective ability to create form from raw materials is disappearing, as is our knowledge of earthly and astral powers. How could the so-called first world survive if there wasn't electricity, climate control, and imported resources like building materials, gasoline, food, and clothing? How many of the daily products we consume do we produce ourselves?

In Carolyn Merchant's book *The Death of Nature*, she examines the scientific revolutions in the sixteenth and seventeenth centuries and science's subsequent effect on people's secular perspective. Here is how she defines nature in her book: "[Nature has] had a number of interrelated meanings. With respect to individuals, it refered to the properties, inherent characters, and vital powers of persons, animals, or things, and more generally to human nature. It also meant an inherent impulse to act and to sustain action . . ."[33]

Merchant asserts that humans are predisposed to take action—our common consciousness leads to collective action, even though our perceptions as to what is acceptable behavior and what is not changes over time. Humankind has worked hard to establish and maintain very meticulous laws so that a common feeling of "order" can be maintained. But within human systems, enforcement and resistance of order go through waves of intensity and focus. Unfortunately, human application of "the law" is haphazard at best—legal "justice" doesn't always coincide with what feels right.

Because of the many oppressive systems around the

---

33 Carolyn Merchant, *Death of Nature: Women, Ecology and the Scientific Revolution* (HarperOne, reprint edition, 1990), p. xix.

world, I believe we need to band together and build a new kind of society. Empires with foundations built upon European colonialism are faltering; the truth about African slavery and the genocide of indigenous nations will no longer be suppressed, and the subjugation of nature cannot continue. The demise of a dominant West will not be graceful, but it is inevitable.

Under the pseudonyms Butch Lee and Red Rover, members and associates of the Weather Underground wrote *Night Vision: Illuminating War and Class on the Neo-Colonial Terrain*, a nineties manifesto on a non-racist, non-sexist, non-homophobic future. Given the Weather Underground's extensive experience confronting oppressive powers from the late sixties onward, their take on such cultural and societal ills was a welcome addition to the activist literary canon.

> *It's critical for us to talk about what race, nation, & gender are, because this is what people are fighting about now. The main political movements—such as Afrocentric nationalism and the women's movement—are about what people think of as biology. Struggling over what is natural and unnatural for humans. Same for nations, too.*[34]
>
> *. . . We're at the turning point where an old reality is giving way to a new reality. Both are still present and true at one and the same time. Combining but increasingly colliding. Especially in our minds.*[35]

Around the same time of *Night Vision's* publication, the

---

34 Butch Lee and Red Rover, *Night Vision: Illuminating War and Class on the Neo-Colonial Terrain* (AK Press, 1998), p. 1.

35 *Ibid*, p. i.

Zapatistas formed in Chiapas, Mexico. The Zapatistas were an autonomous organization of indigenous people with innovative approaches to challenge the global elite. The Zapatistas directly confronted the Mexican government with urgent issues vetted by their numerous community councils.

> By harnessing the transformative capacity of social movement, as well as the memories of past struggles that drive it, the Zapatistas are able to identify the future and act on it today. It is a paradoxical temporal insight that was perhaps best summarized by "El Clandestino" himself, Manu Chao, when he proclaimed that, "the future happened a long time ago!"[36]

At a pivotal time in the rapid consolidation of global capital, the Zapatistas, among many others, sparked a change in the air, and this change is charging forward with great force. Old ways are withering—some for better, some for worse. People are organizing in new ways; cultures are not nearly as isolated as they have been in the past. While these developments are not necessarily ideal for everyone, long-distance communication is crucial in this age of global power. Information is available like it has never been before and there are many more Piltdown discoveries on the horizon.

What is truly at stake now are our bodies and minds. Planet earth, outer space, and even our biological makeup are in serious danger. The survival of our species, as we know it, is at stake. Great towers will only stand as long as our deeds match their height.

Reconciling an honest, inclusive history that incorpo-

---

36 El Kilombo Intergaláctico, *Beyond Resistance: Everything. An Interview with Subcomandante Insurgente Marcos* (PaperBoat Press, 2008), p. 9.

rates many perspectives into the dominant historical ortho-
doxy is what Howard Zinn so aptly achieved with *A People's
History of the United States*. Like Zinn, rather than following conventional thought and dominant ideology, we must
now dig deeper into perspectives from around the planet. As
C.L.R. James wrote in *Every Cook Can Govern*, his exam-
ination of Athenian democracy, "History is a living thing. It
is not a body of facts."[37] We need to live history and make
it, and embrace the responsibility to fulfill our species' true
potential.

---

37 C.L.R. James, *A New Notion: Two Works by C.L.R. James* (PM Press, 2010), p.
148.

CHAPTER 2

REDISCOVERY

You're a sacred seed, plant yourself on fertile ground,
Then make your stand.
Whether flower or reed, dig your roots where life can be
    found,
It could be water or sand.

There was Wanchese, there was Manteo, and there was
    Skyco too,
They lived as brothers although they came from three
    different nations.
They came of age when the English invaded the Outer
    Banks.

They had three different reactions,
They went three different directions,
They took three different paths,
Paths to find peace, inner peace.

Wanchese, he was angry,
Wanchese was willing to fight,
He put up a forceful resistance,
He fought for what he knew was right.

Manteo felt no boundaries,
He clung to his hope for the good of humankind,
But they showed him a different way
When he gave his power away.

Skyco could see both sides,
So them he unified.

He decided to provide
Leadership for all three tribes.

Their differences came between them and friends be-
*   came enemies,*
But Skyco reminded them of their brotherhood.
Only together could they be free.

America is truly a place of great mystery. Historians are still piecing together pre-European history. The richness of the land has served the invaders and subsequent immigrants well, but the willingness to decimate the indigenous populations and to harness slaves from Africa will certainly always haunt the achievements of the ruling class. Many questions remain regarding America's voracious slave-trading relationship with Africa, and on the subject of continuing relations, Haile Selassie said:

> *The American people can make a significant contribution to guaranteeing that a deep and abiding friendship exists between Africa and the United States of America. Learn more about us; learn to understand our backgrounds, our culture and traditions, our strengths and weaknesses. Learn to appreciate our desires and hopes, our problems, our fears. If we truly know one another, a solid and firm basis will exist for the maintenance of the friendly relations between the African and the American peoples, which—we are convinced—both so ardently desire. You may be assured that there will be no failure in the warm and brotherly response from our side.*[38]

---

38   Haile Selassie I, *Selected Speeches of His Imperial Majesty Haile Selassie I* (One Drop Books, 2000), p. 206.

At a young age, I was exposed to an alternate history of my homeland by a few prominent thinkers. In my undergraduate education I took a course with Howard Zinn; at another school in Boston I attended Noam Chomsky lectures. Both Zinn and Chomsky's shake-ups of the indoctrinated collegiate psyche was desperately needed in the eighties. While Chomsky focused more on current events and America's foreign policy, Zinn pointed to the past. Zinn's book *A People's History of the United States* was widely disseminated among academic institutions and progressive bookstores. It was translated into numerous languages and forced students to reconsider conventionally taught history.

While in college I also listened to and met with Bobby Seale, Angela Davis, Abbie Hoffman, Amiri Baraka (LeRoi Jones), Chuck D, and Alice Walker. When I saw Chuck D speak at Harvard, I couldn't help but think of Malcolm X's historic speeches there in the early sixties. These voices of contemporary social history counterbalance mainstream dogma, and they are essential for figuring out where we are, where we were, and where we are going. Real students of history always need to dig deeper.

TRANSATLANTIC TRAVEL BEFORE COLUMBUS

Why is it so hard for some to believe that there was American contact before Columbus? After all, ancient Egyptian culture was rife with sailing motifs. Even in remote caves in the Sahara Desert there are ancient paintings of boats.[39] Some archeologists and other experts have interpreted such nautical art as Egyptian symbols for the afterlife, suggesting that Egyptians formed death cults in which people sailed to .

---

39 Joseph Ki-Zerbo, *UNESCO General History of Africa, Vol. 1, Abridged Edition: Methodology and African Prehistory* (University of California Press, 1989), p. 292.

their version of heaven. But have these experts not considered that Egyptians may have been sailing around the world, trading in goods and culture, long before Columbus stumbled across North America? As John Malam pointed out in *Exploring Ancient Egypt*, "Travel by boat [there] was part of everyday life."[40]

The Cherokee Nation, before their removal, inhabited large sections of the Southeastern US. This area is in close proximity to where a ship following the ocean's natural current from East Africa might land. Many Cherokee people wore turbans like North Africans, who were Muslim and known for their telescopes and sea travel. And as it turns out, the navigator on Columbus's first voyage was a North African.

It is certain that Columbus's travel route was hatched from a plan carried out in the past. "The Portuguese knew of land to the west even before Columbus sailed. They learnt this from Africans and there are documents to prove it," says historian Ivan Van Sertima in *Early America Revisited*.[41] During his second voyage, Columbus wrote that indigenous people in Haiti told him that "black-skinned people had come from the south-east trading gold-tipped spears."[42] These spears were allegedly identical to spears being used in African Guinea; even the words used for "spears" in both languages were the same.

Ferdinand Columbus, Christopher's son, once said, "My father told me he saw Negroes north of Honduras."[43] Van Sertima states that there are dozens of Europeans who re-

---

40 John Malam, *Exploring Ancient Egypt* (Evans Brothers, 1997), p. 20.

41 Ivan Van Sertima, *Early America Revisited* (Transaction Publishers, 1998), p. 149.

42 *Ibid*, p. 150.

43 *Ibid*, p. 150.

ported seeing or hearing from Africans in the Americas. Ferdinand was right: the Charruas of Brazil, the Jamassi of Florida, and the Caribs of St. Vincent were all pre-Columbian black settlements.[44] As he remarks, "The Africans appeared exactly where the ocean current from Africa takes you."[45]

There is also evidence supporting human contact with ancient South America before there was a Bering Strait. According to scholar Lizzie Wade, "Archaeologists used to think that people walked from Siberia through an ice-free passage down Alaska and Canada, reaching the interior of the United States about 13,000 years ago." The reason this isn't making sense anymore is because in Peru, "radiocarbon dates from charcoal place the earliest human occupation at nearly 15,000 years ago."[46]

My theory is as follows: after the first wave of humanity left Africa and moved through India, people migrated from Australia by sea to the Solomon Islands, Fiji, Samoa, Tahiti, Easter Island, and then to the coast of South America. Van Sertima shows evidence of African contact with America during three different time periods—two by Egypt and one by Mali.

ANCIENT EGYPT'S CONTACT WITH WHAT BECAME SOUTH AMERICA

The Congo Dance of Panama is a lasting cultural expression established by escaped slaves, the Cimarrons, and a surviving indicator of Congo's slavery-era influence on South America. South America's relationship to Africa, however, apparently

---

44   *Ibid*, p. 151.

45   *Ibid*, p. 151.

46   Lizzie Wade, "Traces of Some of South America's Earliest People Found Under Ancient Dirt Pyramid," *Science Magazine*, May 24, 2017.

dates back much further. In fact, the earliest African contact with South America is believed to be in the period of Ramesses II, as suggested by the existence of cocaine in the belly of his mummified remains. This plant, only grown in the Americas, apparently enjoyed widespread usage among Egyptian royalty. Ramesses II reigned from 1301–1234 BCE, according to some sources.

The second period of contact with Africa points to the Olmecs of South America around 1200 BCE. There are significant cultural similarities between the Olmecs and certain African cultures, such as carved stone heads with African features discovered in La Venta, in the present Mexican state of Tabasco. (A rather humungous Olmec stone in Tres Zapotes was dubbed "Joe Louis" by the National Geographic Society and the Smithsonian Institute.)

The Olmec culture predated the Aztecs and Mayas and existed hundreds of years before Moses. According to many historians, it's not clear where the Olmecs originated, but some evidence suggests that Olmec culture was a result of Egyptian influence. In *1491: New Revelations of the Americas Before Columbus*, Charles Mann says their creation as a people was caused by "some spark or incitement, a cultural quickening." From being a people similar to their fellow Mesoamericans, they suddenly "had built and occupied San Lorenzo, the first large-scale settlement in North America—it covered 2.7 square miles."[47]

Van Sertima pioneered the research of an African connection and reported the following: "It has been shown that 'the vertical frame-loom with two warp beams used by the Incas was the same as that used in Egypt in the New Kingdom'

---

47 Charles Mann, *1491: New Revelations of the Americas Before Columbus* (Vintage Books, 2011), p. 237.

(1400–1100 BC) . . . Spindle whorls, also used in weaving, were so identical in Egypt, the Mexican capital of Tula, and in Peru, that 'laid side by side, even an expert can scarcely tell them apart.'"[48]

Van Sertima also discovered "a dozen and more unique and complex Egypto-Nubian rituals with clear antecedence in the Old World, duplicated in startling detail in areas where 'amazingly Negroid' stone heads, terra cotta figurines, Negroid skulls and skeletons, have been found."[49] The artwork of the two cultures have significant similarities, and some complex religious ceremonies are literally duplicated. Perhaps most tellingly, "The double crown in the Egypt-Nubian world grew out of special circumstances. It signified the joining of the two lands, the north and south, Egypt and Nubia."[50] This crown had the bird-and-serpent motif; the bird represented the upper world and the serpent the lower. The crown was worn by Tutankhamen, the eighteenth-century Egyptian pharaoh, among others.

Artwork shows the Olmec kings with the same bird-and-serpent motif. Like the Egyptians, Olmec royalty also sported royal crooks and flails. In ancient Egyptian hieroglyphs, the four Sons of Heru (*Horus* in Greek) represented the four directions—Amest, Hapi, Tuamufef, and Gebhsennuf—with each direction corresponding to a color. The Mayans also had gods representing the four directions, each with a distinctive color.

The Olmecs were undoubtedly a very advanced culture, with three different calendar systems that synced up. Like the Egyptians, they also understood the concept of "0" in

---

48   *Ibid*, p. 127.

49   *Ibid*, p. 120.

50   *Ibid*, p. 100.

math, while Europeans did not understand "0" until the Renaissance three centuries later.

Probably the most befuddling evidence of contact between South America and Africa is the ancient Egyptian map of the western outlines of Africa and the eastern seaboard of the Americas. The Piri Re'is Map, named for the Ottoman Turkish admiral, "was redrawn around 300 BC but belongs to an even earlier period."[51] This map includes the correct latitudinal and longitudinal coordinates between Africa and the Americas. These details were completely unknown to Europeans until the 1700s CE.

ABU BAKARI II'S VISIT FROM MALI

The third period of African contact—the Mandingo voyages from Mali, West Africa—occurred between 1310–1312 CE. Many geographical points in Panama are named for these African voyages. There is also a map from 1448 CE tracing the Brazilian coast and its relation to West Africa. It is inscribed with the correct distance between the two landmasses.

These expeditions were part of the history of Mali, which suggests that Abu Bakari II sent two separate fleets of boats across the Atlantic. This is corroborated in the Arabic documents *Al-Qalqashandi* and *Masalik el Absar fir Mamelik el Amsar*.[52] "When Mansa Musa, the most famous of the Mandinga emperors of Mali, stopped in Cairo on his way to Mecca in 1324, he reported that his brother, Abu Bakari II, who had preceded him, had launched two expeditions to discover the limits of the Atlantic."[53]

Mali, in its heyday, was known for cities like Timbuktu

---

51   *Ibid*, p. 121.

52   *Ibid*, p. 19.

53   *Ibid*, p. 22.

and Djenne, centers of commerce and learning, celebrated for the peacefulness of their streets at night. The entire area at that time was able to build on the centuries of development by a great social and economic regime. By the time of Mansa Musa and Abu Bakari II in the early 1300s, urban advancement and international trade were booming.

This was after the time of the great Sundiata, king of old Mali, whose history has been primarily parlayed through oral traditions. The name *Mali* means *free*. The establishment of his Mandinka state began in 1230 and lasted until around 1600. Ghana, its predecessor, had split apart, so the Mandinkas were free to establish their independence. They were economically powerful because they had strong trading ties. With this economic opportunity to establish their global power, Mali expanded its influence greatly by managing terminals for the various caravans sweeping across North Africa. The caravans came down below the Sahara to Timbuktu, Djenne, and Gao, along the Niger River. These routes continued through Sokoto to Benin and the Gulf of Guinea. They later became the routes for the European slave trade, where rum was imported and humans were exported.

Africa had longstanding outlets on the Atlantic seaboard, especially in the period of Mansa Musa. Basil Davidson wrote in *Lost Cities of Africa* that "Edrisi, an Arab nobleman of Andalusia [Islamic Spain from 750–1492], who wrote for the Norman King of Sicily in the middle of the twelfth century, has a reference to Atlantic voyages which seem to have reached the Canaries; while Abulfeda (1273–1332) speaks of voyages round the world, which he describes as a sphere,"[54] likely referring to the voyages of Abu Bakari II.

---

54 Basil Davidson, *The Lost Cities of Africa* (Back Bay Books/Little, Brown and Company, 1987), p. 74.

With an incredible home base to launch from, Mansa Musa and his brother had the potential to accomplish greatness in many fields, including world exploration: "With Timbuktu or Djenne as their intellectual centers, they had wide contacts with the outside world."[55]

The trading center next to Lake Chad, Kuka, gave birth to the Songhai tribe, which is where present-day Chad, Niger, Nigeria, and Cameroon all meet. The Songhai tribe established a dynasty around 300 CE, and their capital was later moved to Gao. Za el Yemeni, who established the long line of Songhai kings, was a Hebrew originally from Yemen. This was the time of ancient Ethiopia's conversion to Christianity,[56] when Constantine and the Roman Empire took control of the religion in Europe.

Rudolph Windsor, in his book *From Babylon to Timbuktu*, pieces together the history of these ancient African Hebrews, flaunting their significance: "The Arabs, Moors, and the Sudanese writers attribute to the ancient black African Hebrews the establishment of the first empires, 'the erection of the first public buildings in the country, the construction of the first canals and irrigation systems, and the institution of a social economic regime which still survives in all Saharan communities.'"[57] The Jewish ruler of Mali had extensive knowledge of this kind of development. Jewish tribes had been driven westward into North Africa and then down below the Sahara by many different conquerors throughout history. The Jews in Africa even spoke the ancient Canaanite language, which eventually morphed into the Hebrew language of the ancient biblical scriptures.

---

55 *Ibid*, p. 78.

56 See Chapter 9, "Sweet Somalia."

57 Rudolph R. Windsor, *From Babylon to Timbuktu* (Windsor Golden Series, 1969), pgs. 89–90, citing Nahum Slouschz, *Travels in North Africa* (Philadelphia: The Jewish Publication Society of America, 1927), p. 344.

By the time Ghana ascended as a power, the region was rife with highly skilled professionals. The population possessed a vast storehouse of knowledge and ability.[58] The region that became Ghana had twenty-two different kings by 622 CE. The name of the region at the time was Aoukar. It became *Ghana* to celebrate this longer line of kings. Ghana was their title, literally meaning *War Chief*.

The fifteenth Za prince took Gao in 1009 CE. During his reign he converted to Islam, although many of the nation's inhabitants remained Jewish. Abu Bakari was the leader of the Almaravides, who invaded Ghana from the northwest in the early 1000s CE. By 1076, Abu Bakari took over in Gao, allowing the king to stay in power. Ghana eventually split apart due to various invasions, and Mali and Songhai filled the power vacuum. Then, of course, came the Europeans.

Today, the Dogon tribe in Mali demonstrates the direct link to the scientific achievements of the early Mali and Songhay empires. Their diagrams of the Sirius star system show more than the naked eye can see. In *Ages of Gold and Silver*, John G. Jackson details how the Dogon knew about the rings of Saturn and the four principle moons of Jupiter, in addition to realizing that the planets revolve around the sun, that the earth is round, and that the Milky Way galaxy has a spiral structure.[59]

THE EUROPEAN INVASION OF NORTH CAROLINA'S OUTER BANKS

Rastafari culture, which encourages an active and open path to learning, strengthens one's capacity for self-realization by

58 *Ibid*, p. 90.

59 John G. Jackson, *Ages of Gold and Silver and Other Short Sketches of Human History* (American Atheist Press, 1990), p. 203. He cites Hunter H. Adams III, *African and African-American Contributions to Science and Technology* (Portland, Oregon: Portland Public Schools, 1987), p. 60.

propagating a well-rounded historical perspective. It also incites a deep repulsion to colonialism, power-dominance over others, and ecological destruction. Colonial mentality, which supports these aforementioned dynamics, is chalked up as wickedness. In Rasta culture, the idea of "Babylon," by way of the Psalms, refers to these counterproductive tendencies.

With mystical elements like "Word, Sound, and Power," and the "Do-Good" beat on Nyahbinghi drums, Rastafari people work to heal the planet. Connections are made with others around the globe through the power of language and the universalizing force of music. Gone are the barriers if we can dance and sing together, even when we have opposing viewpoints. The Rastafari movement's vibrant cultivation of a Living Truth (carrying the past and future into the present) compelled me to inquire into Europe's initial invasion of what we now know as America. I especially wanted to learn more about what it was like before the Europeans came.

When the British arrived on the east coast of what the indigenous people called Turtle Island, they came upon three allied Algonquian nations—Chowanocs, Weapemeocs, and Secotans. According to most historians, the nations along North America's Atlantic seaboard, from present-day southern Maine to North Carolina, shared a similar cultural heritage and spoke a common "Algonquian" language. The Secotans split time between mainland North Carolina and the Outer Banks. The Chowanocs and Weapemeocs dwelled permanently in mainland towns along the rivers. In *500 Nations*, Alvin M. Josephy Jr. provides a window into what it looked like from a European perspective: "It was a world of beauty and plenty. Carefully tended gardens surrounded each town, providing bounteous harvest of squash, two varieties of beans, pumpkins, sunflowers, amaranthus, tobacco, and three strains of corn that sometimes produced two crops a year."[60]

The first reported European contact with North America was in July 1584. Two small British ships, financed by Sir Walter Raleigh, landed at Hatarask Island in what is now North Carolina. Raleigh, called "the greatest Lucifer that hath ever lived in our age" by his contemporaries,[61] was well known for promoting tobacco in England. Granganimeo, the head chief of the Secotans, happily allowed his people to trade with the English: "The trade was conducted with enthusiasm and goodwill on both sides, and Granganimeo in a show of friendship delivered a vast supply of food to the ships."[62]

Granganimeo also received interlopers at Roanoke Island, his hometown just north of Hatarask. Wanchese and his friend Manteo (referred to in the song at the beginning of this chapter), a relative of the chief, accompanied the ship as it explored the barrier islands to explain the Secotan language and culture to the British. Wanchese and Manteo got along so well with the British that they eventually returned to England with the colonizers. But when they came back to their country a year later, they found a different kind of relationship emerging between the two cultures.

The goodwill between the Native Americans and the Brits quickly deteriorated. A British commander stationed on the Outer Banks ordered his soldiers to burn Native American villages and crops for the alleged crime of a stolen cup. The inhabitants tried to explain to the commander their philosophies regarding common property, but when the Brit-

---

60 Alvin M. Josephy Jr., *500 Nations: An Illustrated History of North American Indians* (Knopf, 1994), p. 184.

61 Richard Dale, *Who Killed Sir Walter Ralegh?* (History Press, 2011), p. 51.

62 Alvin M. Josephy Jr., *500 Nations: An Illustrated History of North American Indians* (Knopf, 1994), p. 187.

ish did not listen, the Native Americans faced the wrath of their visitors. Their worst nightmares were now coming true.

"GONE TO CROATAN"

England's first settlement in the Americas was on Roanoke Island in 1587; Manteo from the Croatan tribe was a member of it. The settlement became known as the "Lost Colony" because of its mysterious disappearance. Ten days after its colonization, the ship that brought the Brits to the North American coast traveled back to England to gather supplies. But because of the war with Spain, the British were not able to return to Roanoke Island until three years later. John White, the governor of the Roanoke settlement, was on the supply ship that left for England, and when he and the others finally returned, the group of 117 colonists had vanished: the only trace they left were the words *Gone to Croatan* carved into a tree.[63] The Croatan was a Native American tribe near Roanoke Island and had likely assimilated the colonists. Reports from the early 1700s confirmed European genetic traits were present in the tribe.

This was a surprising start to what became a very different colonization trend in the immediate future. King James's Virginia Company had its sights on the whole East Coast, depositing pilgrims at Plymouth and Jamestown. I assume their goal was not to assimilate with the indigenous nations. King James was the first king of both England and Scotland, and he authorized and financed the English translation of the Bible from Greek and Hebrew. "Monarchy," he is quoted as saying, "is the greatest thing on Earth. Kings are rightly called gods since just like God they have power of life and

---

63 Hakim Bey, *T.A.Z.: The Temporary Autonomous Zone, Ontological Anarchy, Poetic Terrorism* (Autonomedia, 1991), p. 116.

death over all their subjects in all things. They are account-able to God only, so it is a crime for anyone to argue about what a king can do."[64]

Ironically, the Christians who sought to force their reli-gion and culture on Native Americans eventually modeled the US government after the Iroquois Confederacy. The Iro-quois at this time were a six-nation federation comprising the Seneca, Cayuga, Onondaga, Oneida, Mohawk, and Tuscarora. They were located in what is now New England, but over time they expanded south and west. The Iroquois Confeder-acy lasted until the American Revolution, when the British ceded their land to the colonists.

PYRAMIDS IN THE MISSISSIPPI RIVER VALLEY

The Spanish were the first Europeans to carry out expedi-tions into North America during their conquest of South America in the 1500s. Reportedly somewhere between fif-teen and nineteen million inhabitants were slaughtered in the Spanish's quest for gold. Various European conquests led to countless exterminations of indigenous communities, not only from senseless violence but also from illnesses and viruses that wiped out entire tribes.

The first European to make a North American cross-country trek was Cabeza de Vaca. Tony Horwitz writes that de Vaca's journey "made Lewis and Clark's expedition, three centuries later, look like a Cub Scout outing by com-parison."[65] By de Vaca's account, many of the native peoples took pity on him and his team for their hardship. He recalls

---

64   André M. Slade and Katarína Križáni, *Where to from Here: Cognition* (Xlibris, 2014), p. 122.

65   Tony Horwitz, *A Voyage Long and Strange: Rediscovering the New World* (Picador/ Henry Holt & Co., 2008), p. 121.

them weeping for his group when they were found in a desperate state after being shipwrecked. Native Americans also enslaved de Vaca and his people for more than a year.

They had set sail on an expedition headed by Panfilo de Narvaez and their fleet reached the coast of Florida near Tampa Bay in 1528. They crossed the mouth of the Mississippi fourteen years before de Soto did. In 1534, de Vaca found himself deep in west Texas. His search for the fabled Seven Cities of Cibola, with the promise of gold and intrigue, was a symbol for the potential for wealth and power promised in North America. The first member of de Vaca's expedition team to see the Seven Cities was Estevanico, a North African.

Estevanico, originally from Morocco, served as de Vaca's translator and scout, and he ended up developing a strong rapport with the native people. In a later trip to the continent, Estevanico "gathered an entourage of some three hundred natives and began carrying a gourd hung with bells and feathers."[66] Previously, "an entourage of several thousand Indians began trailing the [group], reverently asking them to blow on and bless food and drink."[67]

North America had many distinguished cultures by the time de Vaca arrived. Pyramid-shaped ruins ran along the banks of the Mississippi River and up to the Great Lakes, snaking east of the Ohio River and West Virginia's northern panhandle. The largest pyramid was found at Cahokia, in present-day Collinsville, Illinois. The pyramid is oriented to the sun on the spring and fall equinoxes and the Serpent Mound in Ohio is aligned with the sun on the summer solstice. According to Charles Mann, "Native Americans may have been in the Americas for twenty thousand or even thirty

---

66 *Ibid*, p. 131.

67 *Ibid*, p. 127.

thousand years."[68] At the site of Cahokia, "a group of Indians coalesced sometime before 800 AD."[69] In their heyday, "from about 950 to about 1250 AD,"[70] in addition to building pyramids, they worked with textiles, copper ornaments, and dyed cloth. They also fashioned sheets of mica, which came from the southern Appalachians, into silhouettes of hands, bird claws, and other animals. At least twenty thousand people lived in the immediate vicinity of Cahokia. The dynasty started to grow in the 700s AD. Their temple complex covered fourteen acres, including 120 mounds.

The biggest pyramid at Cahokia is over one hundred feet high, and the similarities with Egypt are astounding. And this is "a four-level earthen mound bigger than the Great Pyramid of Giza."[71] Despite the significant difference in building materials, the precision between the two cultures' architecture is unbelievably exact in its directional orientation. Unfortunately, the mounds built by the Hopewell in Newark, Ohio, became a golf course. Only the Great Circle, over a thousand feet in diameter, has been preserved, with the Eagle Mound at its center.

The Adena were a woodland culture in current Ohio, whose coalescence "lasted from about 800 BC to about 100 BC."[72] It is believed that they were the first to establish agriculture, and their mounds were primarily burial mounds. This distinguishes them from other native cultures in South America who built only temple mounds. A pipe in the form

---

68   Charles Mann, *1491: New Revelations of the Americas Before Columbus* (Vintage Books, 2011), p. 196.

69   *Ibid*, p. 290.

70   *Ibid*, p. 295.

71   *Ibid*, p. 288.

72   *Ibid*, p. 294.

of a human figure, unearthed in Ohio in 1901, is one of the more striking finds. In all, 136 pipes were found there.

The successor society to the Adena is now called the Hopewell culture and first appeared in Illinois. Throughout their history they relocated to Indiana, Ohio, Michigan, Wisconsin, Iowa, and Missouri. These highly advanced cultures came to an end not very long before the first Europeans ventured into the north. The great period of the temple builders was past, but parts of their legacy were preserved among the tribes that followed them.

In *An Indigenous Peoples' History of the United States*, author Roxanne Dunbar-Ortiz reports that Cahokia had a larger population than London at the time, as well as technology capable of building impressive architectural monuments "in the shape of gigantic birds, lizards, bears, alligators, and even a 1,330-foot-long serpent." Citing Charles Mann's book *1491: New Revelations of the Americas Before Columbus*, Dunbar-Ortiz also highlights the fact that "their influence had spread throughout the eastern half of the North American continent through cultural influence and trade,"[73] impacting the societies of the Cherokee, Chickasaw, Choctaw and Muskogee Creek, Seminole, and Natchez nations.

NATIVE AMERICAN RASTAS

Today in the United States, most major cities have a visible and sizable Rasta presence. Reggae music populates many radio stations, podcasts, and music stores; one can even hear Rastas reasoning on a bustling street or observe dreadlocks and Rasta colors on people of all shapes and sizes. Surprisingly, many Native American people have also adopted Rasta-

---

73 Roxanne Dunbar-Ortiz, *An Indigenous Peoples' History of the United States* (Beacon Press, 2014), p. 23–24.

fari culture. Why would people with such strong indige-nous traditions absorb a foreign culture? In *Arise Ye Mightly People*, Terisa Turner frames this phenomenon: "Rastafari has, in its globalization, been taken up by some groups of indigenous people in their struggle to take back alienated land and to protect nature and natural resources. It is also one nexus through which some indigenous peoples link up with intellectuals who recognize that global survival has, as its prerequisite, the enforcement of an end to ecological destruction."[74]

Josh LittleJohn, a colleague of mine, once recounted an experience he had with the Havasupai (or Supai) tribe who live in a reservation in the Grand Canyon. His description of the place was vivid—a clear blue river juxtaposed against the harsh brown desert. As he descended into the remote reserva-tion, he heard reggae music in the distance. He was surprised to find these people, with such a rich and original culture, embracing reggae's symbols and pulsating soundtrack. As Josh told me: "I had not heard about the affinity for Rasta culture before going there . . . We would be walking through the canyon and hear reggae music in the trees somewhere and smell ganja. I definitely wanted to go find the source of both at the time but caution kept me from being invasive."

Another person to find fascination with these Grand Canyon Rastas was Chris Blackwell, the founder of Island Records, who was making a film about Bob Marley in the early 1980s. He had commissioned long-time reggae chron-icler Roger Steffens to take a film crew to the Grand Can-yon to interview these Havasupai Rastas. They heard about "tribes people, their hair coiled into dreadlocks and dressed

---

74 Terisa E. Turner and Bryan J. Ferguson, *Arise Ye Mighty People!: Gender, Class and Race in Popular Struggles* (Africa World Press, 1994), p. 5.

in traditional Rasta colors of red, green and gold, [who] invoke the name of Jah in their conversations."[75]

Because of the veneration the Havasupai had for Bob Marley, Steffens brought Bob's mother, Cedella Booker, and the Wailers' organist, Tyrone Downie, along with the film crew. Unfortunately, the footage never surfaced and there was disdain among the Supai for those who had abandoned the project. In "Transnational Popular Culture and the Global Spread of the Jamaican Rastafarian Movement," Neil Savishinsky commented on the Havasupai's relationship with Rastafari:

> Not only do the Havasupai listen to reggae, but some even play it as well. Many also smoke ganja and strongly identify with the anti-Babylon (anti-Western) sentiments expressed in the lyrics of numerous Jamaican reggae songs.
>
> The Havasupai claim that reggae music was first introduced into their community by three Indians from California who brought with them a large collection of Bob Marley cassettes. Over the years enthusiasm for the music grew among the younger members of the tribe to the point where in the early 1980s reggae and Rasta culture came to play a major role in Havasupai life.[76]

As far as Rastafari's unifying element, Terisa Turner states that "as the oneness of the world market becomes more pronounced, the oneness of the exploited, unwaged and waged,

75 Roger Steffens, "Rastas of the Canyon: Take a Trip to the Indian Reservation Where Bob Marley and Reggae Music Reign Supreme," *High Times Magazine* (Feb. 1993), p. 46.

76 Neil J. Savishinsky, "Transnational Popular Culture and the Global Spread of the Jamaican Rastafarian Movement," *New West Indian Guide* 68, No: 3/4, 1994, p. 264.

becomes more tangible."[77] Rastafari's symbols and principles live as significant commonalities in a varied global movement within popular culture. "In sum, new forces have adapted Rastafari into a different and even more potent world social movement," says Turner.[78]

Casper Loma-Da-Wa, of Hopi and Navaho descent, has examined the occasional difficulties between Rastafari and Native Americans, especially when it comes to reggae. Some tension has arisen over tales of gun-slinging and Wild West imagery in the music. Loretta Collins Koblah explains this fascination as an "enthusiastic Jamaican consumption of filmic narratives of cinema cowboys, posses, sheriffs and 'Indians.'" Koblah says that this imagery wrongfully overlooks the devastating impacts of the Manifest Destiny and westward migration. Loma-Da-Wa suggests that the reggae fascination with Euro-Americans moving west disregards and offends many indigenous peoples throughout the world.

Still, Loma-Da-Wa also finds many positive commonalities within his dynamic heritages. Koblah highlights the shared captivation with anciency:

> The idea of anciency implies purity, righteousness, and a natural state in which human beings are in touch with their full intuitive powers and innate intelligence, where they are in harmony with the natural world . . .
>
> By selecting this centrally important roots ideology from reggae and merging it with Hopi beliefs that the Hopi have been designated as divinely gifted caretakers of the mesas surrounding land from ancient times to the

---

77 Terisa E. Turner and Bryan J. Ferguson, *Arise Ye Mighty People!: Gender, Class and Race in Popular Struggles* (Africa World Press, 1994), p. 4.

78 *Ibid*, p. 16.

present, Loma-Da-Wa asserts a counterclaim: in the "New World," in fact, the Hopi is the "original landlord." This counterclaim is offered as not only a harmonious counterpoint to Rasta claims but also as a defense against encroachments on Hopi land and lifeways by the US government and the Navajo (Dine). However, like the reggae singer who claims spiritual wisdom as an "original man" who is able to convey a sense of truth, justice, the divine, and natural wholeness because of his connection to the earliest moments of creation, Loma-Da-Wa also establishes his authority to accurately and insightfully "chat culture" and history on the microphone.[79]

The deep relationship between music and history continues to be fluid. The Internet has spawned a new generation with global proclivities, and their connections to history and social interaction extends beyond the boundaries of nation and continent. Gateways have opened to greater research like never before, and I expect we'll see many more people's histories.

---

79 "Ribbon Shirts in Rasta Colors: Native American Syncretic Musical and Visual Strategies of (Jamaican) Resistance in the Lyrical Imagery, CD Jacket Art, and Performance Costuming of Hopi/Dine Reggae Singjay Casper Loma-Da-Wa," *Image [&] Narrative* online magazine, Issue 11, May 2005.

CHAPTER 3

EVERY CLOVER

Every I is an I, from the bottom to the Most High.
Every clover you step over is a companion to our lives.
Every flower has the power that flows through you
* and I.*
Like the motion of the ocean, we flow with the surge of
* life.*

Earth is alive! She is spontaneous,
But oh, she's tired, she's been beguiled
By her children who've lost sight of their own humanity,
* reality,*
Lost the ability to see with the one I that can see.

Every star near and far, a necessary number for the hu-
* man race,*
The chemical balance of the universe leaves nothing to
* waste.*
The more microscopic the topic, the more it looks like
* outer space,*
This world that's before us is a pretty amazing place!

RASTAFARI: WHERE I-NIVERSAL CULTURE
MEETS ECONOMIC GLOBALIZATION

Rastafari can help sort through the smokescreen of daily life because of the historical perspective that informs our livity (lifestyle). If we follow Rastafari livity, we are better attuned with the goods we consume, our relationships with our neighbors, the hair on our bodies, and the grass in our yards—we are attuned to *every clover*. Having a reverence for life's intricacies is so important. Nature's function in our lives governs how we relate to everything else—what we fear, how we love, and what role religion and/or spirituality plays. A symbiotic relationship with nature is true wealth, and its worth in our culture sorely needs to be reexamined. As Haile Selassie said, "The forests, the rivers, the mountains and the plains constitute wealth."[80] Without seeing our cosmic interconnectedness, without respect for each other—every I—and for nature, we are destined to repeat the same cycles that have plagued humanity for centuries.

Rastafari Ites (heights) shine a light into the darkness and allow a pathway for humanity to progress forward more peacefully. Through the heartbeat rhythm of the Nyahbinghi, even Rastafari's drumming is attuned to the human form. Its message is positive, its wisdom vast; Rastafari holds a key to healing the human condition—individually *and* internationally—while repairing our relationship with nature.

A few years ago I had the chance to travel to Jamaica in order to cultivate interconnectedness with co-ops in the Southeastern US. My personal goal was to help the Jamaican people receive their due, especially the Rastas, because their culture has given me such valuable guidance throughout the years. My interest in working with Rastafari elders materialized while I was living in western North Carolina. A group of colleagues and I created the Rastafari Ancient Living Arts and Kulture Festival (RALAK), where we hoped to raise enough money for others to develop a Rastafari trust fund. The idea behind the fund was simple: Rastafari symbols

---

80 Haile Selassie I, *Selected Speeches of His Imperial Majesty Haile Selassie I* (One Drop Books, 2000), p. 454.

should be treated as the intellectual property of the Jamaican Rastas. Funds would be accumulated from the profits of products utilizing the imagery of Rastafari. A board would then vote on ways to disperse the funds throughout the Jamaican Rasta community.

The Rastafari Millennium Council worked to spearhead this mission and we were set to help. That meant our group had visits and conference calls with people like Ras Michael from the foundational Sons of Negus reggae band, Bunny Wailer, representatives of Stephen Marley, and other prominent Rastafari scholars and advocates. According to the Rastafari Millennium Council, their vision is to "speak with ONE VOICE for all those that professes the Rastafari Faith, in order to promote, protect, and preserve the sacred legacy of the Rastafari Indigenous Culture worldwide." They have been very effective in fostering cooperation between the various mansions of Rastafari in Jamaica, as well as networking with Rasta communities worldwide. One of their primary focuses has been "to advocate and negotiate with appropriate bodies in order to further the interests of the Rastafari Communities, in matters of Repatriation, Reparations, Cultural Heritage projects, Human Rights and Welfare, Intellectual Property, and the like."

In my area we formed the Black Mountain/Asheville Rastafari Collective (BMARC), which was started when Ras Sela Juda Fari and Empress Iffiya Seales moved to North Carolina with their family. Ras Sela was involved with the RMC, and Empress Iffiya had been raised in the Nyahbinghi mansion. In 2008, Empress Iffiya became their first female chairperson. Because of the Theocracy Reign Ivine Order of Nyahbinghi's patriarchal history, her appointment was a significant accomplishment.

Due to my work with Ras Miles Jacob Marley and the Rastafari UniverSoul Fellowship Prison Ministry, it was inevitable that our paths would cross once they moved to the small town I was living in. It was particularly gratifying whenever I interacted with Binghi Irie Lion, Empress Iffiya's father, and Ras Michael, because I wanted to be more exposed to the wisdom elders like them carry. By way of the festival, we also had contact with other movers and shakers within the Rasta movement, including elder Ras I-RICE and members of the International Development of Rastafari (IDOR). The festival was a gathering of Rasta visionaries from all over the US and Jamaica.

While in North Carolina, Haile Israel from Ras Michael's band and Binghi Irie Lion accompanied us to the Alexander Correctional Institution to visit with Rasta inmates. Because of my growing connection within the Rasta community, I also joined Ras Sela on a trip to the United Nations to meet with Under-Secretary General Francis Deng, a descendent of Mandinka royalty. He was South Sudan's first ambassador to the UN and had taken a keen interest in Rastafari because, as he said, it was the fastest-growing religion in Africa. He contacted us because his son had come to our festival, where one of the defining events was an interfaith reasoning, featuring a panel with many different spiritual perspectives.

After the following year's festival a group of us met with H.I.H. Prince Ermias Sahle Selassie, Haile Selassie I's grandson and president of the Crown Council of Ethiopia. Jake (John) Homiak, director of the National Anthropological Archives at the Smithsonian Institution, arranged our meeting. We discussed hosting the RALAK Festival in Addis Ababa, Ethiopia, so that it could coincide with the restoration of the statues of H.I.M. Haile Selassie I, which were taken down during the 1974 Ethiopian civil war. Prince Ermias was extremely appreciative that Rastafari communities like ours continued to celebrate the great emperor.

RASTAFARI, CO-OPS, AND ORGANICS IN JAMAICA

I arrived in Jamaica on the eve of their 2016 presidential elections and was met at the Kingston airport by Nkrumah from the Source Farm Foundation. One immediate thing that struck me while driving to their ecovillage was the appropriation of the term *Jah* by the Jamaican Labour Party on their campaign billboards. Jah is the Rasta term for the Most High (or God), and it was evident that the political party was trying to appeal to voters with Rastafari's pervasive cultural influence. Rastas, however, are quick to disavow what they call "poli-tricks." They have been repeatedly persecuted on their own island by the same political forces that were now trying to use their symbols to appeal to voters. With the recent decriminalization of marijuana, many Jamaicans are worried that the forces of appropriation will swallow up the ganja industry.

I was invited to Jamaica by the Source Farm Foundation and the Jamaican Sustainable Farm Enterprise (JSFE) to potentially establish multiple co-ops to spread organic produce and natural food products throughout the island. Together we wanted to create direct links between Jamaican farmer and retail co-ops with cooperatives in the US. I had recently seen the masterful documentary *Life and Debt*, a film that examines the International Monetary Fund and World Bank's involvement in decimating the Jamaican economy. Because many Jamaicans had been repeatedly ripped off by the "establishment," developing co-ops would instill sustainable economic opportunities for local communities.

As I traveled through the island and met with people, I witnessed the primary cooperative tendencies coming together: organics, sustainability, gender equality, transparency, and accountability. I would actually argue that the organic movement would not be as internationally prevalent if not for Rastafari people speaking truth to power and sending out their messages with such an inviting soundtrack. Rastafari has always been about sustainability, collective security, the interconnectedness between all living things, and a reverence for nature.

A primary reason for establishing cooperative roots within Jamaica was reiterated in my JSFE materials. "The people of Jamaica and the greater Caribbean region," the materials said, "have long been buffeted by manmade and natural disasters that have left them in a state of economic, social, and environmental crisis." While the intricacies and specifics vary on each island, they've all been subject to the same predatory international bankers, which has affected everything from their agricultural practices to the prices they're able to get for exports. Spreading cooperative and organic practices in Jamaica is so important because there, "people are vulnerable due to national dependency on unaffordable, less healthy, imported food, lost skill sets needed to produce certain crops without expensive chemical inputs, and natural disasters that wipe out farmers' crops with regularity."

Clearly, democratic control over local Jamaican industries could be a big help in turning these problems around. The JFSE materials also highlighted the internal dynamics at play in the region where I was headed:

The Parish of St. Thomas and the other eastern parish of Portland have systemically been the most forgot-

ten and underdeveloped parishes in Jamaica for over a century. Because of the Morant Bay Rebellion in 1865, St. Thomas was labeled as a "troublemaker parish" by government and has suffered from little to no effective representation by both the past and present governments of Jamaica. This neglect has resulted in poorly maintained roads, lack of functional infrastructure, high unemployment, poor living conditions, and a great sense of hopelessness amongst the youth. St. Thomas is a farming parish however, since the liberalization of the banana industry by the European Union and NAFTA all the banana plantations have closed leaving few agricultural avenues for profitable employment in the parish. Many of the people of St. Thomas still rely on small cash crops and seasonal tree crop production for their livelihood, but are only marginally compensated for their crops, with most of the profits going to middlemen and retailers in Kingston and local markets . . .

As evidenced by a grocery store operator I met with who said he was building the Whole Foods of Jamaica, there is an increasing demand for healthy organic food products. JSFE sees this both as a challenge and an opportunity. Their materials identified "a long history of support for clean food and organic agriculture in Jamaica and farmers are thirsty for new effective methods of improving production and distribution. Marketing structures are in their infancy and need direct technical assistance to support their success."

The Source Farm Foundation, based in St. Thomas, Jamaica, is JSFE's primary partner and has been busily working to provide training to counteract the global economic forces that have been squashing Jamaica's economy. One of their more prominent programs helps farmers understand the benefits of organic agriculture and permaculture practices. The Source Farm Foundation also helped fuel the Ujima Natural Farmers Market, Jamaica's first organic farmers market.

One of my tasks in Jamaica was to help farmers with their postharvest processing so they could enhance their offerings at the market. When a local market gets flooded with one crop, the competition is fiercer than it needs to be. If farmers organize into co-ops, or at least become willing participants in an overall strategy, they can grow complementary crops and sell what they need to keep themselves afloat.

HUMANKIND'S SUBJUGATION OF ITSELF

In a chapter titled "Rastafari and the New Society," Terisa Turner points to research done by Maria Mies that reveals the synchronicities of historic tendencies:

> [Mies's] integrative methodology links the historical emergence of European science and technology, and its mastery over nature, to the European witch killings and the attendant deskilling and economic marginalization of women. And both the persecution of the witches and the rise of modern science are linked to European slave-based triangular trade and the destruction of self sufficient, autonomous economies in Africa and the new world. As capitalism developed in the 20th century, and especially after WWII with the more pronounced unification of the world market, first world women were concentrated in the work of reproduction and consumption. At the same time, third world women were forced to produce cheap

export and wage goods, according to specific demands of
colonial and imperial capital.[81]

The current global economic system is primarily parasitic in nature. It would be a mistake to blame this strictly on the Europeans, although in our current era the so-called first world is typically at fault. Power brokers in developed and developing nations participate in unethical behavior and work together to generate suffering around the world, and much of this suffering is tied to global economic inequality.

Oxfam crunched the numbers and their results don't look good: "In 2015, just 62 individuals had the same wealth as 3.6 billion people—the bottom half of humanity. This figure is down from 388 individuals as recently as 2010." While there has been an increase of more than half a trillion dollars for the wealthy elite, "the wealth of the bottom half fell by just over a trillion dollars in the same period—a drop of 41 percent."[82]

> *One of the key trends underlying this huge concentration*
> *of wealth and incomes is the increasing return to capital*
> *versus labour. In almost all rich countries and in most*
> *developing countries, the share of national income going*
> *to workers has been falling. This means workers are cap-*
> *turing less and less of the gains from growth. In contrast,*
> *the owners of capital have seen their capital consistently*
> *grow (through interest payments, dividends, or retained*
> *profits) faster than the rate the economy has been grow-*

81   Terisa E. Turner and Bryan J. Ferguson, *Arise Ye Mighty People!: Gender, Class and Race in Popular Struggles* (Africa World Press 1994), pgs. 18–19.

82   Oxfam International Staff, "An Economy for the 1%: How Privilege and Power in the Economy Drive Extreme Inequality and How This Can Be Stopped," *Oxfam International* (January 2016), p. 2.

ing. Tax avoidance by the owners of capital, and gov-
ernments reducing taxes on capital gains, have further
added to these returns. As Warren Buffett famously said,
he pays a lower rate of tax than anyone in his office—
including his cleaner and his secretary.[83]

The Oxfam report also illuminates an alarming economic trend occurring in Africa: "Almost a third of rich Africans' wealth—a total of $500 billion—is held offshore in tax
havens. It is estimated that this costs African countries $14
billion a year in lost tax revenues. This is enough money to
pay for health care that could save the lives of four million
children and employ enough teachers to get every African
child into school." Shielding wealth from tax regulation is
one of the key factors preventing any kind of trickle-down
economic effect.

Contending with similar forces in 1964, Haile Selassie I
worked hard to stem the trend. At the Organization of African Unity (OAU) Summit in Cairo that year, he argued that
"long-established patterns of trade are not easily or quickly
reoriented." He implored the dignitaries to not be fooled into
thinking that this fact could be lost on them in the remaking
of their future. "But let us, at the same time, toil with all our
strength to alter them," he said.[84]

A United Nations–sponsored study reported in 2014
that this type of inequality "matters not only for those at the
poorest end of the distribution, but for society as a whole—
as it threatens social cohesion and hampers social mobility,
fueling social tensions that can lead to civil unrest and polit-

---

83 *Ibid*, p. 4.

84 Haile Selassie I, *Selected Speeches of His Imperial Majesty Haile Selassie I* (One Drop Books, 2000), p. 270.

ical instability. Large income disparities can even undermine democratic values."[85]

Many people will no longer stand for this corruption. Economic starvation encourages rebellion and this trend cannot continue without formidable resistance. But before such a resistance can coalesce, an effective analysis of global trade is necessary.

GLOBALISM AND DEPENDENCE: ONE-CROP ECONOMIES

Every island in the Caribbean Sea has been manipulated by European colonial powers, so when the World Bank and IMF took their turn at interfering with the Caribbean economies, it was simply a transfer of power. In the early eighties, Don Rojas served as the press secretary under Maurice Bishop in Grenada, around the same time the US invaded that nation under President Ronald Reagan. The pretext for the invasion was the apparent civil unrest following Bishop's assassination, which many believe was the result of a covert CIA operation. In his book *One People One Destiny: The Caribbean and Central America Today*, Rojas offers a local perspective in response to the economic and social difficulties that come with what he calls "imperialist bullying."

Instead of giving back to the countries whose resources were sapped, the US often coerces them with propagandist aid. In the guise of the savior, the US imposes economic programs in developing countries that function in the "totality of US interests," not through force, but through "influence."[86]

---

85   United Nations Development Programme, "Human Development Report 2017, Sustaining Human Progress: Reducing Vulnerabilities and Building Resilience," p. 39.

86   Susan George, *How the Other Half Dies: The Real Reasons for World Hunger* (Penguin Books, 1986), p. 47.

Susan George argues that this political framework has created and furthered world hunger:

> The West has tried to apply its own conceptions of "development" to the Third World, working through local elites and pretending that the benefits showered on these elites would trickle down to the less fortunate, especially through the wholesale application of Western-inspired and Western-supplied technology. These methods have not produced a single independent and viable economy in the entire Third World—and in fact were not meant to. "Development" has been the password for imposing a new kind of dependency, for enriching the already rich world and for shaping other societies to meet its commercial and political needs.[87]

Many people are left to their own limited devices, merely grasping for survival. Like the parish of St. Thomas in Jamaica, the whole island of Haiti seemingly had to pay for its successful slave uprising between 1791 and 1804.[88] In his book *In the Parish of the Poor*, former Haitian president Jean-Bertrand Aristide explains how "aid" agencies actually destroyed his country's development. He observes that "the same free foreign rice the pastor feeds to the peasant's children is being sold on the market for less than the farmer's own produce." Local elites benefit in the marketplace because they have freely acquired food to sell. "Would it not be better . . . to force the landholders to increase the peasants' pay . . . to help the peasant learn to organize? Isn't this a

---

87   *Ibid*, p. xvii.

88   See *The Black Jacobins: Toussaint L'Ouverture and the San Domingo Revolution* by C.L.R. James (Vintage, 1989).

better way to stop the children's cries of hunger forever?"[89]

US foreign policy continually leads to subtle and not-so-subtle disasters. In Walter Rodney's book *How Europe Underdeveloped Africa*, he discusses the historical "contradiction between the elaboration of democratic ideas inside Europe and the elaboration of authoritarian and thuggish practices by Europeans with respect to Africans." [90] "There is a type of false or pseudo integration," he writes, "which is a camouflage for dependence. In contemporary times, it takes the form of free-trade areas in the formerly colonized sections of the world. Those free-trade areas are made to order for the penetration of multi-national corporations."[91]

Rodney continues to elucidate the West's denial of interconnectedness: "In the short run, European racism seemed to have done Europeans no harm, and they used those erroneous ideas to justify their further domination of non-European peoples in the colonial epoch. But the international proliferation of bigoted and unscientific racist ideas was bound to have its negative consequences in the long run."[92]

Although Walter Rodney was writing in 1972, he already saw how NAFTA, the WTO, and the TPP would transform the world economy. "Free trade" is a slick misnomer for a controlled economic environment where powerful governments and corporations create rules to suit their own ends. At the 1964 Organization of African Unity Summit, Haile Selassie I spoke about these effects:

---

89 Jean-Bertrand Aristide, *In the Parish of the Poor: Writings from Haiti* (Orbis Books, 1990), p. 68.

90 Walter Rodney, *How Europe Underdeveloped Africa* (Bogle-L'Ouverture Publications, 1972), p. 89.

91 *Ibid*, pgs. 111–112.

92 *Ibid*, p. 89.

Neo-colonialism today takes two forms: economic and political. We recognize that economic dominance is not only often the more difficult to eliminate, but often serves as the entering wedge for political domination. We further recognize that, given the history of our continent, and the conditions under which we came to freedom, it is not unusual that, despite our best efforts, the economic independence which we seek is long and difficult in coming.[93]

Ethiopians have always fervently valued their independence, and this ethic has been passed on to Rastas. Rastafari emphasizes self-reliance and inspires its followers to lead productive and self-sufficient lives. Because Rastafari is not about escapism, adherents are aware of current events and how they relate to their personal lives. The constant presence of reasoning among Rastas keeps dialogues progressive rather than dwelling on the past. Neil Savishinsky identifies these traits in his essay "Transnational Popular Culture and the Global Spread of the Jamaican Rastafarian Movement":

By encouraging young people to take an active interest in the land through their establishment of small-scale agricultural projects, by promoting the use of ganja as a substitute for alcohol and other more harmful drugs, and by creating an appreciation and demand for locally manufactured goods, Rastas in Trinidad have served as a positive social force, especially among the island's poor.[94]

---

93 Haile Selassie I, *Selected Speeches of His Imperial Majesty Haile Selassie I* (One Drop Books, 2000), pgs. 269–270.

94 Neil J. Savishinsky, "Transnational Popular Culture and the Global Spread of the Jamaican Rastafarian Movement," *New West Indian Guide* 68, No: 3/4, 1994, p. 263.

A BRITISH CUP OF INDIAN TEA WITH CARIBBEAN SUGAR

Plantation-style mono-crop systems across the world have decimated many peoples' ability to be self-sufficient. In *Sweetness and Power: The Place of Sugar in Modern History*, Sidney Mintz considers the tremendous influence British trade with India and the Caribbean islands had on its society:

> *The first sweetened cup of hot tea to be drunk by an English worker was a significant historical event, because it prefigured the transformation of an entire society, a total remaking of its economic and social basis. We must struggle to understand fully the consequences of that and kindred events, for upon them was erected an entirely different conception of the relationship between producers and consumers, of the meaning of work, of the definition of self, of the nature of things. What commodities are, and what commodities mean, would thereafter be forever different.*[95]

The developed world needs to reexamine its relationship with imported goods in order to produce a commerce system that benefits more people. Although a growing number of consumers are recognizing the benefits of buying local, political forces continue to perpetuate a dependence on mass production. In *Wild Fermentation*, Sandor Katz acknowledges the role government and the economic elite have in determining mass production:

> *The enormity of the economic and cultural changes wrought to the entire world by the mass production and*

---

95 Sidney W. Mintz, *Sweetness and Power: The Place of Sugar in Modern History* (Viking Penguin Inc., 1985), p. 214.

global trade of chocolate, coffee, and tea cannot be over-stated. These stimulants recognized today as addictive substances were "the ideal drugs for the Industrial Revolution," according to ethno-botanist Terence McKenna . . . Europe married them to sugar and they became that important new mass commodity's marketing partner.[96]

The colonial powers and their private partners dominated this trade explosion and subsequently seeds of dissent were planted everywhere they went. Not only were these nations and companies plundering proud people and their land, they were manipulating their own constituents who were hopelessly dependent on the crumbs of their spoils. As long as the ruling elite could demonize the people they plundered, the gentry felt justified in cracking the whip to keep the slaves in line.

St. Thomas in Jamaica was an early colonial landing spot for the British, who took over the former Spanish rule of the colony. The Spanish had set up minor cattle ranches and agriculture developments, but the British established full-blown plantations. The Plantain Garden River Valley, where I met with farmers on my trip to Jamaica, had originally been home to sugar estates and banana plantations. More recently, it had been turned into an agro park, land set aside for farmers to grow mostly onions for export. At the time I was there things hadn't gone well. Here's what Source Farm had to say about these developments:

Small farmers have had many challenges over the past decade due to the liberalization of the Banana Industry

---

96 Sandor Ellix Katz, *Wild Fermentation: The Flavor, Nutrition, and Craft of Live-Culture Foods* (Chelsea Green Publishing, 2016), p. 29.

by NAFTA's ruling, the closing of the Eastern Banana Estates and the recent failure of the onion crop at the PGR Agro Park. It is our hope that with the introduction of the Jamaican Sustainable Farm Enterprise Program, we will be able to re-energize agriculture in Eastern St. Thomas while we address a number of environmental challenges around sustainable land practices and address issues of climate change, which is impacting the region.

Chuck Marsh, a coordinator of JSFE and site plan creator for the Source Farm Ecovillage, organized my visit to Jamaica. I first met Chuck at Earth Haven Ecovillage, near where my kids spent the majority of their early childhood. One morning during my Jamaican stay, Nicola "Coda" Shirley-Phillips—the Source Farm Foundation's executive director—and I headed down to the PGR Agro Park to find a specific group of farmers she had been communicating with. PGR is southeast of the Blue Mountains, where the majority of Jamaican coffee is grown. Coda instructed me before I left the US, however, that if I wanted good coffee I should bring my own. It turns out many local Jamaicans can't get the famous Blue Mountain coffee their country produces. It's almost entirely exported. I made sure to bring them extra Ethiopian coffee from my co-op in Asheville.

As we met with the farmers, their cautious approach with us was understandable given their experience with exploitation, although they made it clear that Coda was trusted. Because a few of the farmers appeared to be Rastas, I cited Haile Selassie I's nod to cooperatives as a viable alternative to the neoliberal policies of the IMF and the World Bank. His Imperial Majesty stated that the "co-operative movement has long been known throughout the world, and We

Ourself have on numerous occasions urged Our people to join increasingly in co-operative enterprises. Co-operatives must, ultimately, play a highly important role in the growth of Our economy, and no time can be lost in availing ourselves of the benefits to be derived from them."[97]

According to the *Jamaica Observer*, the nation's farmers had already been exploited by the mismanagement of the Agro Invest Corporation, which "resulted in the loss of a projected $50 million worth of onions." Meanwhile, the PGR Agro Park is "among those touted to produce Jamaica out of debt under the International Monetary Fund (IMF) agreement." I assured the farmers that our goal in assisting them was to form an "iron sharpen iron" kind of relationship; this is a phrase borrowed from Proverbs 27:17 that was also incorporated into a popular song by the reggae band Culture.

Despite my best efforts, I saw that words only went so far with these stoic farmers; they needed to witness actions to believe our words. For a fruitful relationship with the US cooperative sector, we needed to make sure to follow through in a meaningful way.

JOURNEY TO MAROON TOWN, AND A NYAHBINGHI GROUNDATION IN PORTLAND

On March 1, 2016, the 120-year anniversary of the Battle of Adwa—a defining moment in the Ethiopian fight against Italian colonialism—Nkrumah and I left Source Farm at 5:45 in the morning on what turned out to be a very long day. We purchased some hearty fish soup with okra, carrots, and scallions from a street vendor outside of Lyssons before traveling

---

97   Haile Selassie I, *Selected Speeches of His Imperial Majesty Haile Selassie I* (One Drop Books, 2000), p. 520.

to a rendezvous with Binghi Irie Lion, Maxine Stowe, and noted Jamaican journalist Dickie Crawford.

The day before, Coda and I had met with Jah B (Bunny Wailer) and Maxine Stowe. We discussed how the SFF could successfully work with them to establish an ecovillage like Source Farm as somewhat of a retirement home for aging Rasta elders on land Jah B had purchased. They were also hoping it could be a tourist destination for African Americans. At that meeting, Maxine let us know about a ceremony the next day where the Maroon community was going to be receiving a delegation from Sierra Leone which was interested in rekindling and acknowledging their shared lineage and history.

The Maroons from Jamaica had been a formidable foe to the British colonial encroachment, and their resistance resulted in a peace treaty. I was acquainted with some of their history and learned about their fearless female leader, Queen Nanny. This was a resistance movement comprised largely of escaped slaves. After fending off the British, they became an integral part of Jamaica's history despite existing independent of the Rasta community.

During my post–high school forays into Washington, DC's vibrant African American cultural centers, I frequently visited Georgia Avenue, near Howard University. Georgia Avenue housed Soul Vegetarian, a vegan eatery run by the African Hebrew Israelites; Delights of the Garden, a raw food deli; the House of Khamit, an Afrocentric bookstore run by scholars who regularly engaged in insightful discourse; and the House of Knowledge, a three-story dwelling that held Revolution Books (a Socialist-oriented Afrocentric bookstore), a health food store, and a Nation of Islam outpost. After the closure of many of these businesses, Ethiopian filmmaker Haile Gerima, who made an important film called *Sankofa* starring reggae singer/poet Mutabaruka, opened a café nearby, and the African Hebrew Israelites opened a health food store called Ever Lasting Life (run by Onam, a close friend of mine from the DC punk scene). On the same side of the street was the long-standing Blue Nile Herb Shop where the tonic I regularly bought there—wood root tonic—was made from a Maroon recipe. Reading the label gave me my first introduction to Maroon culture, and I was able to follow up with research in books I bought at the House of Khamit and the many street vendors in the area.

That day in Jamaica, as Nkrumah and I drove to Maroon Town and back, we swerved around both slow and speeding cars, trucks, bikes, pedestrians, and goats. After driving through Spanish Town, we met up with Maxine and Dickie and headed to Bog Walk to pick up Binghi Irie Lion. Binghi Irie and I had a chance to catch up in the car. As previously mentioned, he had traveled to a North Carolina prison with the RUF Prison Ministry and me. Binghi Irie's insight during our visit was pivotal for Rasta inmates to overstand the true nature of the faith and its history. That day in the car I looked on as Rastas from the street celebrated his presence when we drove by.

During the trip, passing mountains that overlooked Ocho Rios and the coastal town of Falmouth, I saw my first cruise ship since arriving to Jamaica. It was a startling site after being immersed in local communities. The floating country club was an intrusion, to say the least, on the rich vibes the locals were living. As I knew from growing up in DC, tourists serve an industry that may or may not be needed, and their presence was not entirely welcome.

We were heading to Montego Bay, also a tourist destination, which provided a stark contrast with St. Thomas. Driving through the city, we passed the Hyatt Hotel, Holiday Inn, and Hilton, virtual compounds flanked by massive golf courses and chlorinated swimming pools. Tourists are warned by these hotels not to venture out among the *natives*. We drove past the hotels through to lunchtime. We stopped at a grocery store so Dickie could visit an ATM, and Nkrumah treated us to soup he bought from a street vendor. We were on our way.

We headed into the hills above Montego Bay to Maroon Town, also known as Flagstaff and Trelawny Town. The Maroons settled in these hills in 1690; escaped slaves fled there and waged guerrilla warfare against the colonial regime. It was in 1739 that the British were forced to sue for peace due to the decimation of their forces.

The ceremony was already underway when we got to Maroon Town; the Maroons were singing their anthem. Among them was Chief Michael Grizzle and Mama G (Gloria Simms). The Sierra Leone delegates were on the walkway above, which overlooked the Maroon domain. Once out of our car, Binghi Irie was already chatting with Rastas there. Meanwhile, Michael Grizzle was talking with his diverse set of guests—he had invited delegates from the Muslim and Rasta communities. Along with another Maroon "paramount chief," Michael Grizzle kept the proceedings in order, welcoming a group of students from a primary school nearby and two university professors from the US. Mama G was also a vital participant—her powerful presence was a reminder of the many strong women elevating Jamaican culture.

It had already been a long day, and Nkrumah and I were now charged with getting Binghi Irie to the Groundation in Portland on the east side of the island. After partaking in a local treat from some women across the street called "Blue Drawers" ("Du Ku Nu," as called by the locals), which was like a banana and coconut dumpling wrapped in banana leaf, we headed out along the northern coast. Our only stop was for some food in Buff Bay, after listening to a radio show on Mellow FM along the way.

When we finally got to Portland for the Groundation, I was determined to only stay for a short while, although this was an important event for Nkrumah and me. Unfortunately, the Groundation was taking place fifteen hours after we had left Source Farm and we still had to drive home. I was surprised at how inclusive the Groundation was. What surprised me most was how graciously we were welcomed. After all, we were two *baldheads*—my dreads were just starting to form again and Nkrumah was a Jamaican with no apparent allegiance. It didn't seem to matter—we were just more branches on the tree.

CHAPTER 4

JOHN BROWN

He laid down his life to fight for freedom
For the African slaves who were taking a beating.
At Harpers Ferry there were ten killed in the raid,
Out of twenty-two men, just five escaped.

He defended Kansas from a Missouri invasion,
He pushed Lincoln to push emancipation,
He planned to conquer Virginia to tip the balance of the
    South,
Inciting the slaves in every state to come out.

He was a hero in Kansas
Just before the Civil War,
He had beaten back a Southern invasion
So the slaves could find their way
To the land of their freedom.

He was a hero in Kansas,
He had a plan to place arms in the hands
Of the slaves who would join him
To make their so-called masters pay their way
To the land of their freedom.

The Union soldiers had an anthem about his trek,
The chorus lives on in the Battle Hymn of the Republic.
"Glory, glory, hallelujah," he fought so others could be
    free.
"His soul is marching on," as Lincoln signed his decree.

*Throughout history, it has been the inaction of those who
could have acted, the indifference of those who should
have known better, the silence of the voice of justice when
it mattered most, that has made it possible for evil to
triumph.*[98]
—Haile Selassie I

I n the early 1990s, I moved back to DC from Boston to
join a band some friends had recently formed, Rain Like
the Sound of Trains. Along with my Boston comrade
Linc, I also wanted to help restart the DC chapter of Food
Not Bombs, an organization that served meals to the homeless. In Boston, the anti-Apartheid movement had contributed to my interest in activism, as had the local Food Not
Bombs chapter.

Eric Weinburger, the Food Not Bombs anchor, had participated in the Civil Rights Movement by going on Freedom Rides. Despite all the important activist work he had
accomplished in his life, he was humble and I truly enjoyed
collaborating with him. Howard Zinn wrote about him in the
introduction to the book *Food Not Bombs* by C.T. Butler and
Keith McHenry:

> *I had met [Eric Weinburger] . . . on the road from Selma
> to Montgomery, Alabama, in the great civil rights march
> of 1965, and again in 1977, in another march, this time
> of anti-nuclear activists, into the site of the Seabrook nu-
> clear power plant.*
>
> *Now another dozen years had elapsed, and he was
> with Food Not Bombs. I thought these Food Not Bombs*

---

98 Alter Wiener, *From a Name to a Number: A Holocaust Survivor's Autobiography* (AuthorHouse, 2007), p. 206.

folk are carrying on the long march of the American people, moving slowly but inexorably toward a livable society. The message of Food Not Bombs is simple and powerful: no one should be without food in a world so richly provided with land, sun, and human ingenuity. No consideration of money, no demand for profit, should stand in the way of any hungry or malnourished child or any adult in need. Here are people who will not be bamboozled by "the laws of the market" that say only people who can afford to buy something can have it.[99]

Joining forces with the Food Not Bombs members to cook soup and distribute discarded food amounted to a profound atmosphere of camaraderie and debate. Working with them gave me my first experience in consensus decision-making, and together we read and discussed a lot of books about anarchism.

Once Linc and I restarted the DC Food Not Bombs chapter, we were able to work with other activists within the DC punk scene, a community I was still heavily connected with. Our collaboration gave birth to the Beehive Collective, which opened a storefront on U Street in Northwest DC. The bottom floor operated as a free thrift store, the next flight up had a record store and information shop, and the top floor housed the kitchen, where we prepared meals for Food Not Bombs. We hosted many discussion groups, various activist circles, and jumpstarted the DC chapter of the Anarchist Black Cross political prisoner support group. We were devoted to studying the work of revolutionaries from the sixties and seventies so we could put our activity into historical

---

99 Keith McHenry, *Hungry for Peace: How You Can Help End Poverty and War with Food Not Bombs* (See Sharp Press, 2012), p. 7.

context, but also so we could learn from our predecessors' accomplishments and mistakes.

John Brown, an iconic figure from the mid-1800s, stood out as a white man who put his life on the line for black freedom. Because most of us were white, Brown served as a potent inspiration. And while we were not interested in waging an armed insurrection, we were interested in working in tandem with black movements in order to further their aims by leveraging our white privilege.

WARRIOR OF THE LORD AND OF GIDEON

"It is infinitely better that this generation should be swept away from the face of the earth, than that slavery shall continue to exist,"[100] John Brown once said. The magnitude of the slave trade—the horrible human cost—deeply perturbed Brown, whose ardent abolitionism was intended to stir an ongoing revolution. Conquering the system really meant conquering the mentality that allowed it to flourish. In some ways, Haile Selassie I's perspective in Ethiopia mirrored this sentiment.

Brown, a conductor on the Underground Railroad that channeled free slaves north and to Canada, decided to take heavier action to end slavery. The symbolic significance of his brave but botched Harpers Ferry takeover helped steer national events in a new direction. History has shown that Brown's raid electrified the nation and spurred a "great fear" in the South, provoking a crisis that had a role in launching the Civil War. Brown was a keystone: mere months after his demise, Southern secession began, and Lincoln eventually followed suit and freed the slaves on January 1, 1863, barely four years after Brown's hanging in Virginia.

---

100   Michael Daigh, *John Brown in Memory and Myth* (McFarland, 2015), p. 138.

Just before the Civil War, Southerners had invaded Kansas in search of runaway slaves. John Brown and his small band retaliated with a deadly strike, where they killed slavery sympathizers. They pressed on into Missouri, where they freed eleven slaves. Brown justified this as retaliation for the Marais des Cygnes massacre. In 1858, proslavery adherents had killed five settlers in Kansas who opposed the extension of slavery to the state. According to scholar Stephen Oates, "Brown asserted that he had 'forcibly restored' eleven human beings 'to their *natural; & inalienable rights*' at the expense of only one white man 'who fought against the liberation.'"[101]

John Brown believed peaceful emancipation was impossible, so he attempted to seize the US weapons arsenal at Harpers Ferry to conquer Virginia, incite slaves throughout Appalachia, and instigate a powerful change in human history, almost biblical in proportion. He even set up a Provisional Constitution, which read: "Slavery, throughout its entire existence in the United States, is none other than a most barbarous, unprovoked, and unjustifiable war of one portion of its citizens upon another portion—the only conditions of which are perpetual imprisonment and hopeless servitude."[102]

"When I strike, the bees will begin to swarm, and I shall want you to help hive them," Brown told Frederick Douglass at the time.[103] Douglass, however, refused to follow him. Harriet Tubman joined his cause, but was too sick to attend the Harpers Ferry incident. Douglass later lamented his decision,

101 Stephen B. Oates, *To Purge this Land with Blood: A Biography of John Brown* (University of Massachusetts Press, 1984), p. 263.

102 David S. Reynolds, *John Brown, Abolitionist: The Man Who Killed Slavery, Sparked the Civil War, and Seeded Civil Rights* (Alfred A. Knopf, 2005), p. 251.

103 W.E.B. Du Bois, *John Brown* (G. W. Jacobs, 1909), p. 297.

stating that "John Brown's zeal in the cause of freedom was infinitely superior to mine. Mine was as the taper light; his was as the burning sun. I could live for the slave; John Brown could die for him."[104]

The Jamaican Maroons were one of Brown's main inspirations for holding his position in Virginia. He and his partners intended to use the mountainous region as a stronghold, and one of his cohorts in Kansas verified that he had "studied all the books on insurrectionary warfare he could find, paying special attention to the Maroons of Jamaica and Toussaint L'Ouverture's liberation of Haiti." A friend of Brown's said that he "knew the story of Jamaica and Haiti 'by heart,'" and noted abolitionist Thomas Wentworth Higginson said that "part of Brown's plan was 'to get together bands and families of fugitive slaves' and 'establish them permanently in these [mountain] fastnesses, like the Maroons of Jamaica and Surinam.'"[105]

In the end, only twenty-one men willingly followed Brown to Harpers Ferry in an effort to liberate slaves. Ten were killed in the raid, including two of Brown's sons, Watson and Oliver; seven were hung, including Brown himself; five escaped, including his son Owen. Dangerfield Newby, who was born into slavery, was the first raider to be killed. Many consider Newby to be the inspiration for Quentin Tarantino's film *Django Unchained*.

Dangerfield had been freed by his white father, but he had a wife and seven children held in slavery in Warren-

---

104 Brando Simeo Starkey, *In Defense of Uncle Tom: Why Blacks Must Police Racial Loyalty* (Cambridge University Press, 2015), p. 36.

105 David S. Reynolds, *John Brown, Abolitionist: The Man Who Killed Slavery, Sparked the Civil War, and Seeded Civil Rights* (Alfred A. Knopf, 2005), p. 107.

ton, Virginia. His wife's master had told him that for the sum of $1,500 he could buy his wife and his youngest baby, who had just started to crawl. Dangerfield earned that amount of money and went back to Warrenton to purchase his wife and baby, only to have his wife's master raise the price. The free black man then joined John Brown in the hope of freeing not only his wife and youngest baby, but his entire family.[106]

As the nation plunged into the Civil War, marching Union soldiers sung a tune titled "John Brown's Body." "His soul is marching on," they avowed. Brown also inspired the 15,000-line poem of the same name by Stephen Vincent Benet, which decrees that Brown found it "necessary" to "forfeit" his life for the cause of destroying a "wicked, cruel, and unjust" system. More than a century later, the man also inspired the punk-saturated John Brown Anti-Klan Committee.

LIBERATED SLAVES, LIBERATED CONSCIOUSNESS?

After emancipation, newly freed slaves struggled to find true spiritual, cultural, and economic freedom in America. In Jesse McDade's study of Frantz Fanon, subtitled *The Ethical Justification of Revolution*, he pinpoints one of the key reasons slaves in the US were truly never freed:

Freedom is more than the absence of external restraint; it requires the presence of a liberated consciousness. This consciousness is not another's to give, it is a state of the psyche that must be won. For without a change from within, the changes without are superficial . . . The slave

106   Stephen D. Brown, *Haunted Houses of Harpers Ferry: Regional Ghost Stories* (The Little Brown House, 1976).

*can only overcome his slavery and become fully human
only through a life and death struggle for his freedom.*[107]

Bob Marley echoed an aspect of this sentiment in "Redemption Song": "Emancipate yourselves from mental slavery, none but ourselves can free our minds." These lyrics evoked Marcus Garvey's words: "We must create a second emancipation—an emancipation of our minds."[108]

Gregory Stephens elaborates on the significance of mental emancipation in his essay "Rethinking Mental Slavery, Racialism, and Bob Marley's Legacy." Stephens calls this notion of a "second emancipation" from mental slavery "one of the great ideas in human history." He argues that race-based thinking is a central trait of mental slavery. Interestingly, Stephens writes, Marcus Garvey thought differently. Garvey's nationalist vision facilitated an ethnocentric viewpoint:

Like the Klan, [Garvey] hated mulattoes, as evidence of "amalgamation" or racial impurity. This was quite an irony, considering that it was the biracial Bob Marley who became the best-known international spokesman for Garvey's "Africa for the Africans" philosophy.

What Bob had to say on these matters ought to be a fundamental challenge to black vs. white racial binaries. We find Bob declaring that he was "neither on the black man's side, nor the white man's side, but on God's side." He insisted that Asians and Europeans could also be Rastas. He declared that "Unity is the world's key, and

---

107 Jesse N. McDade, *Frantz Fanon: The Ethical Justification of Revolution* (Boston University, 1970), p. 67.

108 Gregory Stephens, "A Second Emancipation Transfigured? Rethinking Mental Slavery, Racialism, and Bob Marley's Legacy," *JahWorks* (Feb. 6, 2005), p. 1.

racial harmony. Until the white man stops calling himself white and the black man stops calling himself black, we will not see it.[109]

Stephens cites Ralph Ellison and Frederick Douglass when arguing against racial binaries, writing, "We get our appearance (phenotype) through our genes, but our culture is a learned language. To think that we can determine someone's intelligence or culture by their skin color or phenotype is one of the most fundamental forms of mental slavery."[110] Thus, when Marley sang "One Love," sympathizing with "hopeless sinners" and those with thin chances in life, he sought to praise the Lord for guidance under "one love, one heart," appealing to inclusivity, not one-sided liberation.

Still, attempting to be "color-blind" is a mistake. Society has been organized by race theory; powerful systems have devastatingly affected the lives and opportunities of people of color. But because "both slavery and the opposition to slavery were international and 'multiracial' phenomena,"[111] I believe that a united panoply of races can undo this devastation. Reggae artists like Desmond Dekker feel similarly, positing ideas such as, "We must live as one."

Haile Selassie I championed anti-slavery efforts in Ethiopia. During his reign, Italy had leveraged slavery as a means to justify their second invasion in 1935, yet like Selassie I, his predecessors had been working on eradicating the "deeply rooted" tradition.[112] Emperor Tewodros II, who came to power

---

109 *Ibid*, p. 3.

110 *Ibid*, p. 6.

111 *Ibid*, p. 7.

112 Haile Selassie I, *The Autobiography of Emperor Haile Selassie I: King of Kings of All Ethiopia and Lord of Lords, My Life and Ethiopia's Progress Volume II: Addis Ababa 1996* (Frontline Books, 1999), p. 175.

four years before John Brown's raid, made the first attempt to end the practice in 1854, just before his coronation. He outlawed the slave trade, but its pervasive nature made the new law largely untenable because of a lack of enforceability.

Keep in mind that slavery in Ethiopia looked different than slavery in America. In contrast to the Europeans, and especially the Puritans, the Ethiopian Christian ideals helped stem abuse heaped upon slaves, as well as limit their length of servitude. The "Fetha Negast," a legal code compiled around 1240 by a Coptic Egyptian Christian writer, "sought to control and in a sense humanize [slaves] by specifying a number of situations in which the slave owner was obliged to emancipate his or her slave. Market values were to that extent subordinated to moral considerations."[113]

Yet it wasn't until Emperor Haile Selassie I came to power in the 1920s that Ethiopian slavery truly dissipated. His approach was pragmatic, as he felt "it was impossible to uproot such an ancient institution simply by writing laws."[114] The emperor also "feared that a sudden end to slavery would create an influx of a large underclass with no means to support itself; that would have created two million destitute people overnight. Thus, his was going to be a deliberate process including substantive laws and tough enforcement mechanisms that would gradually put the institution of slavery out of commission."[115]

As highlighted in Richard Pankhurst's definitive book *The Ethiopians: A History*, a key moment in Ethiopian history was the Battle of Adwa, which as I have mentioned

---

113 Yelibenwork Ayele, "Slavery in Ethiopia," *African Holocaus* (October 25, 2011), p. 1.

114 Haile Selassie I, *The Autobiography of Emperor Haile Selassie I: King of Kings of All Ethiopia and Lord of Lords, Volume II* (Michigan State University Press, 1994), p. 175.

115 Hanibal Goitom, "Abolition of Slavery in Ethiopia," Library of Congress (February 14, 2012).

is depicted inside the sleeve of Bob Marley's *Confrontation* album. This was when European colonialism was stopped in its tracks. The Ethiopians defeated invading Italians in 1896, thirty-three years after Lincoln's Emancipation Proclamation. According to Molefe Asante, an African American Studies professor at Temple University, the victory catapulted Ethiopia's significance "in the eyes of Africans as the only surviving African State. Ethiopia became emblematic of African valor and resistance" and a "bastion of prestige and hope."[116]

At the time of the Battle of Adwa, African American "buffalo soldiers" created another psychological lift for black Americans. Although glorified in Bob Marley's famous song, the buffalo soldiers' actual relationship with Native Americans at the time contained problematic truths. But Marley was not highlighting the buffalo soldier battles with indigenous people; instead, he was shining a light on the tenacity of people fighting for their needs with tremendous self-determination. Significantly, their liberation came at a cost for the Native Americans.

Ironically, during the Civil War, black troops fighting with the Union fended off Cherokee, Seminole, Chickasaw, and Creek tribesmen who had joined Confederate efforts. The buffalo soldiers served on the ever-shifting front lines during the Indian Wars, which lasted from 1866 to the early 1890s. Their name, a sign of respect bestowed upon them by the Cheyenne, refers to their fierce fighting abilities and the texture of their hair.

Roy Cook challenges the idea that Native Americans

---

116 Molefe Asante quoted in *Pan-Africanism in Barbados: An Analysis of the Activities of the Major 20th Century Pan-African Formations in Barbados* by Rodney Worrell (New Academia Publishing, 2005), p. 16.

exuded respect for "these marauding murderous cavalry units."[117] During the Indian Wars, frontiersmen and soldiers mowed down huge numbers of buffalo in a brutal effort to starve tribes; unfortunately, the buffalo soldiers served that terrible duty, though they did not help commit large massacres of Native Americans.

> *This buffalo soldier only reflected the overall values of the culture in which he struggled for a place, hoping to ally himself with the dominant American group. As historian William Gwaltney, a descendent of buffalo soldiers, said, "Buffalo soldiers fought for recognition as citizens in a racist country and . . . American Indian people fought to hold on to their traditions, their land, and their lives." These were not compatible, harmonious goals that could provide the basis for interracial harmony.*[118]

TULSA, BLACK WALL STREET, AND THE RISE OF A CENTRAL BANK

Even after slavery was abolished in the US, white elites amassed tremendous amounts of wealth due to their continued cheap labor kept in place by the harsh conditions of sharecropping and servitude. In some ways, John Brown's aims had been achieved, because the slaves were in effect freed. But because slaves did not enact their own liberation, society is still shaped today by inequities and biases that have never been adequately addressed.

The multiracial society Brown envisioned is a society much like what Rastafari people have aimed to create. Corporate economic forces, though, just like colonial forces be-

---

117 Roy Cook, "Plains Indian View of the 'Buffalo' Soldier," *American Indian Source.*
118 *Ibid.*

fore them, never heed or facilitate the full aspirations of their workforce. No one in this current economic climate should work for those who generate their capital through exploitation and degradation. No one should endure the lack of a living wage, mandatory overtime, and no health insurance. Yet such is the reality of the modern workforce in the postindustrial era.

The Civil War established the federal government as it is today. The period of economic growth that immediately followed the war is called the Gilded Age (1865–1901), a term coined by Mark Twain and Charles Warner. The Gilded Age was a tax-free time for the so-called captains of industry: Vanderbilt, Rockefeller, Carnegie, etc. This tumultuous period was marked by incredible prosperity for the American upper class, as immigrants from all over the world flooded through Ellis Island providing cheap labor. Like today, economic elites were awarded favor by the US government because of their financial and social prominence. Thus, the informal marriage between private market forces and federal power steered the nation forward; President Franklin D. Roosevelt understood this as a decades-old legacy. "The real truth of the matter," he said, is that "a financial element in the larger centers [of America] has owned the Government ever since the days of Andrew Jackson."[119]

Andrew Jackson, founder of the Democratic Party and Tennessee's first congressman, was elected the seventh president of the United States in 1829, exactly one hundred years before the first Wall Street crash. He was known famously as the "Indian Killer." He enacted policies that seized indigenous peoples' land, handing the ownership off to his pals at

---

119 Elliot Roosevelt, *F.D.R.: His Personal Letters, 1928–1945* (Duell, Sloan and Pearce, 1950), p. 373.

a low price. He likewise signed the Indian Removal Act of 1830 and negotiated the Treaty of New Echota, which led to the "Trail of Tears and Death," as one Choctaw leader put it. The Trail of Tears featured the duplicitous removal of Native Americans, yet it amounted to a great migration of former slaves too. When the Trail of Tears commenced, the Native Americans were forced to abandon one of the most biodiverse regions in the country.

> *This odyssey, during the 1830s and before, the lives of blacks and Native Americans would be linked on the infamous, cruel "Trail of Tears." On long marches under extreme duress and hardship, the trail led to present-day Oklahoma, Kansas and Nebraska. Indian Territory would be split by the creation of the Kansas and Nebraska territories . . . Pressed by rival chiefs, many of the tribes officially sided with the Confederacy. Afterward, many former black slaves, Freemen, were registered as members of the tribes and offered sections of the Indian land allotments. After the government opened Oklahoma for settlement, more blacks came seeking freedom from Southern oppression and for new opportunities in the Promised Land. Of the more than 50 all-black towns, more than 20 were located in the new state, the more prosperous were Boley and Langston.[120]*

In 1908, O.W. Gurley, a wealthy black landowner from Arkansas, helped institute a strong African American economy in Tulsa. Gurley built a rooming house, which later became the home of Vernon A.M.E. Church. The rooming

---

120 "Tulsa Race Riot Report," Oklahoma Historical Society (Feb. 28, 2001), p. vi.

house was "on a muddy trail that would become the Black Wall Street of America. According to B.C. Franklin, Gurley bought 30 or 40 acres, plotted them and had them sold to 'Negroes only.' Attorney Franklin's account of the settlement of Greenwood shattered earlier notions of blacks being forced in a section of town."[121] Oklahoma's racial segregation laws prevented black people from shopping anywhere other than Black Wall Street, so the money from the newly established black townships was funneled back into their own economy. This was happening in other black communities too, in places such as Fort Worth, Texas, and Nashville, Tennessee. But as these black communities were eventually pushed out and relegated to other neighborhoods, the landmarks of black industry and self-reliance were demolished, and effectively erased from history.

I learned about hidden histories such as this during my time with the Rastafari UniverSoul Fellowship Prison Ministry. While facilitating Rasta reasoning groups at the Marion Correctional Center in North Carolina, I met a man named Stephen Smith, who at the time had been incarcerated for seventeen years in the US penal system. When Stephen was finally released from prison, he promptly enrolled in business classes and joined the board of directors of the food co-op I currently manage. He now lives in the same town as my family and me and is a successful entrepreneur who helps former inmates find job placement. When Stephen heard that I was traveling to Tulsa to participate in a social justice event at the Woody Guthrie Center, he told me to check out Black Wall Street.

I arrived in Tulsa preparing to play music and partici-

---

121 *Ibid.*

pate in panel discussions, but visiting Black Wall Street offered me a much richer experience. As I learned, African Americans created a center of commerce that could have certainly rivaled other contemporary economic hubs in the US. Unfortunately, the racial climate of the country was rife with conflict and violence, and in 1921 Black Wall Street was burned to the ground by whites who believed an African American shoe shiner raped a local white female elevator operator. This resulted in a disturbing sequence of events: the mass arrest and detention of six thousand black citizens, thirty-five demolished and damaged blocks, and more than three hundred deaths in the Greenwood district. Because of Tulsa's vigorous KKK activity, the horrendous crimes went completely unpunished. The event is still the largest massacre of black people on American soil, ever, dwarfing other events like Houston's 1917 Camp Logan riot, where 156 black soldiers mutinied against a racist police force, leading to the death of four soldiers and sixteen civilians. White supremacist society still overtly held the reins at this point in history, and black people suffered the consequences.

Despite lackluster media coverage of these events, poets like Langston Hughes penned writings such as "The Negro Speaks of Rivers," and blues and jazz music ached with social and political hardships experienced by the black community. Marcus Garvey rose to prominence and runner-turned-philosopher W.E.B. Du Bois asked one of the most important questions of his home country: "Would America have been America without her Negro people?"

After the Gilded Age and the turn of the century, successful businessmen in America lavishly expressed their economic prowess. The age of the robber barons was also the era of America's expansion to the West. The Homestead Act of

1862 had given land grants to families for moving westward. Because of this rapid expansion, the Native Americans' "inalienable rights" to their new land was not respected. There was a whole class of robber barons with social connections shaping the structure of a corporate capitalist empire. E.H. Harriman, for example, amassed incredible wealth using Chinese immigrants for cheap labor. Harriman had control of the Union Pacific and Southern Pacific railroads.

Because of capitalism's inherent perpetuation of an underclass, increasing wages could not be sustained long term. These bloating businesses needed the labor to get cheaper for them to grow, and more significantly, they needed a central bank—something we were warned against by our Founding Fathers. (In his letter to the secretary of the treasury, Albert Gallatin, Thomas Jefferson wrote, "I believe that banking institutions are more dangerous than standing armies . . . If the American people ever allow private banks to control the issue of currency . . . the banks and corporations that will grow up around them will deprive the people of their property until their children wake up homeless on the continent their fathers conquered.")

Prosperity for the elites dwindled around 1893. After the gold supply dried up, fifteen thousand businesses closed and five hundred banks failed. Unemployment rose in most industrial cities and mill towns, and prices fell for export crops, causing farmers to suffer financially. Yet, to impose a central bank in the US there needed to be a crisis. Hence the great financial panic of 1907, followed by a great propaganda campaign supporting a centralized bank. "The [JP] Morgan interests took advantage to precipitate the Panic of 1907, guiding it shrewdly as it progressed," reported Fredrick Allen in *LIFE Magazine*. The Federal Reserve Act, written by bankers, passed in 1913 despite significant protests by senators and citizens alike. Massachusetts Senator Henry Cabot Lodge called the Federal Reserve "highly dangerous, especially where there is political control of the board." He continued to describe the Federal Reserve as menacing to the welfare of the American People "in the highest degree."

Woodrow Wilson, who was elected president in 1912, heavily supported the Federal Reserve, and the Federal Reserve Act became law while he was in office. Later he wrote, "[Our] great industrial nation is controlled by its system of credit. Our system of credit is privately concentrated. The growth of the nation, therefore, and all our activities, are in the hands of a few men . . . who necessarily, by the very reason of their own limitations, chill and check and destroy genuine economic freedom."[122]

In 1921, the year of the Tulsa race riot, Congressman Charles Lindbergh wrote, "Under the Federal Reserve Act, panics are scientifically created. The present panic is the first scientifically created one, worked out as we figure a mathematical equation" (see Lindbergh's *The Economic Pinch*). Congressman Louis McFadden was poisoned at a banquet before he could push for an end to the Federal Reserve. He was quoted as saying that the panic "was a carefully contrived occurrence. Industrial bankers sought to bring about a condition of despair, so that they might emerge the rulers of us all."

COOPERATIVE ECONOMICS

Cooperative economics provide positive and progressive financial opportunities to their beneficiaries while simultaneously facilitating fair enterprise, self-reliance, and bottom-up

---

122 Woodrow Wilson, *The New Freedom: A Call for the Emancipation of the Generous Energies of a People* (Doubleday, Page and Company, 1913), p. 185.

participatory economics (traits recognizable on Black Wall Street). I currently work in the cooperative sector at a co-op grocery store in Asheville, North Carolina. The importance of cooperative economics appears to be more evident the more local businesses adopt the model. Businesses and individuals all over the world are discovering that political independence is tethered to economic independence. People of conscience need to make choices about where to spend their money. As the DC band Fugazi once sang, "Never mind what's been selling, it's what you are buying." People vote with their money. Consumers can shop at a corporate chain that circulates money out of a community and depresses local wages, or consumers can support interconnected businesses that have hands-on, fair, and transparent relationships with growers, distributors, sellers, and consumers.

Haile Selassie I made the assertion, "If the wealth of a person cannot be for the general welfare, what would he gain for himself and his offspring but grudge and hatred?"[123] Returning to power after World War II, Selassie I wanted to further develop Ethiopia's infrastructure. On the subject of cooperatives, he examined the larger principle and pointedly stated, "There is no peace without cooperation."[124] "Co-operation and unity," he later said, "are the sources of respect."[125] Cooperative economics are a nonconfrontational way to wage the kind of revolution everyday people need. In 1976, Haile Selassie I presented these theories to the Council on Foreign Relations in New York:

---

123 Haile Selassie I, *Selected Speeches of His Imperial Majesty Haile Selassie I* (One Drop Books, 2000), p. 456.

124 H.I.H. Prince Ermias Sahle Selassie, *The Wise Mind of H.I.M. Emperor Haile Selassie I* (Frontline Books, 2004), p. 103.

125 Haile Selassie I, *Selected Speeches of His Imperial Majesty Haile Selassie I* (One Drop Books, 2000), p. 467.

So long as far-sighted people like yourselves, in each nation and community, recognize the essential interdependence of all peoples in the economic field, as indeed in other areas of human endeavor; and so long as they realize that there are enormous mutual benefits to be derived from co-operative economic efforts, there is reason to hope that the world economic situation will improve and undoubtedly at a greater pace than ever before.[126]

In 1959, Haile Selassie I proclaimed he would "set up groups of experts who will give [the people] advice and counsel in co-operative farming and trading."[127] He testified to their positive results in 1971 at an annual nationwide address, saying that the cooperatives "established in various parts of the country have proved to be of considerable service and assistance to a large number of rural communities. It is our fervent hope that these cooperatives will continue to grow and expand."[128]

The International Cooperative Alliance is a nonprofit association established in 1895 to advance the cooperative social enterprise model. It has 305 member organizations from 105 countries. Together these cooperatives represent nearly one billion individuals worldwide. This alliance provides a global voice and forum for knowledge, expertise, and coordinated action for and about cooperatives, ranging from banking, agriculture, insurance, health, and housing. It includes both consumer cooperatives and worker cooperatives.

---

126 *Ibid*, p. 155.

127 *Ibid*, p. 458.

128 Haile Selassie I, *Important Utterances of H.I.M. Emperor Haile Selassie I* (One Drop Books, 2000), p. 281.

The ICA holds that "retail food cooperatives have a long and successful history" in the US. From the pioneering of nutritional labeling to the introduction of natural and organic foods, co-ops "have played a leading role in bringing healthy innovations to the markets they serve."

Dr. Jessica Gordon Nembhard's *Collective Courage: A History of African American Cooperative Economic Thought and Practice* offers significant historical insight and highlights the importance of co-ops. Gordon Nembhard provides the most modern and comprehensive history of African American co-ops, building upon W.E.B. Du Bois's seminal but outdated *Economic Cooperation Among Negro Americans.* Gordon Nembhard details the work of such stalwarts as Du Bois, Marcus Garvey, Fannie Lou Hamer, Ella Jo Baker, the Black Panther Party, and the Nation of Islam, relating a story of black pride, industriousness, aspiration, resilience, community-mindedness, and entrepreneurship.

This incredibly rich history has been neglected, partially because in the oppressive era of Joseph McCarthy in the middle of the twentieth century, many co-ops removed the word "cooperative" from their name for fear of being associated with communism. Yet in 1966 the Black Panthers evoked the word in number four of their infamous "10-Point Platform." Under the heading "We Want Decent Housing Fit for the Shelter of Human Beings," they demanded that "the housing and the land should be made into cooperatives so that our community, with government aid, can build and make decent housing for its people."[129]

We should extol pride in America's mutually beneficial co-op legacy, because such systems spur community mind-

---

129 Terry Bisson, *On a Move: The Story of Mumia Abu-Jamal* (Litmus Books, 2000), p. 46.

edness, forge trustful bonds, and help foster an equal playing field among men and women in the workforce. As Gordon Nembhard pointedly argues, "Economic participation in cooperatives increases the capacity to engage in civic and political participation and leadership development. Cooperatives also increase women's economic participation, control over resources and economic stability, with important implications."[130]

The Cuban Revolution of 1959 would likely have gratified John Brown, who studied the Maroons of Jamaica and the Haitian Revolution. In an incredibly pivotal time for the organization of international capital, Haiti fought and claimed independence from France in 1804 (although the US did not officially recognize the country's independence until 1862). European communities at the time were responding to the need for local control over their essential resources, as massive industries were taking over the reins of commerce. Food was certainly a focus, and the cooperative model of community economic stability was desirable.

The first co-ops in their modern form started in Europe as the result of dependencies that came with the Industrial Revolution. Masters of industry were building and expanding cities, which created new population centers without land for people to grow their own food. For the first time, many were entirely dependent on stores and landlords. The powerful were able to profit off of low-quality food and housing. Workers, consumers, farmers, and producers needed a way to protect their interests, so they banded together.

Store owners were notorious for adding filler to products like flour to increase their profits. Meanwhile, workers were of-

---

130 Jessica Gordon Nembhard, *Collective Courage: A History of African American Cooperative Economic Thought and Practice* (Penn State University Press, 2014), p. 25.

ten paid in store credit. They had no choice but to patronize their own oppressors because they had no other means for sustenance and shelter—that is, until they came up with a new idea:

> Groups of people began experimenting with various methods of providing for their needs themselves. They decided to pool their money and purchase groceries together. When they purchased goods from a wholesale dealer and then divided them equally among themselves, they were surprised at the savings and higher quality of products they were able to obtain.[131]

England's foundational cooperative was established in Rochdale in 1844. A year prior to its opening, Charles Dickens journeyed to Lancashire to witness how life was lived in England's industrial north. Dickens was taken aback by the terrible conditions he saw, especially when comparing such conditions to wealthy areas of England. What he saw influenced him to write A Christmas Carol; meanwhile, the Rochdale pioneers were meeting just eleven miles away.

According to Patricia Cumbie's "The Rochdale Pioneers' Message to the Future," "One of the things that consumed the political thoughts of the Rochdale Pioneers was their lack of democratic power. Only people who owned land had the right to vote at that time, and the Rochdale Pioneers felt this injustice deeply." They were concerned about empowering those who could not vote, and they necessarily felt the "ideals of cooperation" could be "a step toward introducing democracy to a reluctant society. They built housing

---

131 "The History of Co-ops," Co+op, Stronger Together, 2016.

cooperatives in order to claim they were landowners and be able to vote . . . While the Pioneers strove for political democracy themselves, they also wanted economic democracy. They understood what you control is what you have invested locally."[132]

132 Patricia Cumbie, "The Rochdale Pioneers' Message to the Future," CDS Consulting Co-Op Library, January 30, 2009.

CHAPTER 5

DREAMS

Dreams
a poem by Marilyn Buck

These dreams do not rise from clear blue days
They're of mirages of fresh breezes
They flow from blood running into furrows
Where hope lies underground awaiting nourishment
These dreams call from dark cells
Where hearts guard the Flame of Liberation
These dreams will come to life in hands
Firmly grasping, hands firmly grasping

Hoes, hammers, drums, guitars, and other hands
Those small hands of our children
Taking their steps toward the future
Hoes, hammers, everyone join another's hand
These dreams will come to life

L ike John Brown, Marilyn Buck stands out to me as a true revolutionary. In Marilyn's terms, she was a "European anti-imperialist" working with the "New Afrikan Liberation Movement" to thwart a common enemy: the international empire. When governments fail to adequately serve their constituents, naturally confrontation occurs. In Marilyn Buck's case, she was incarcerated in the US from 1985 up until a month before her death in 2010. She was initially convicted for her participation in the 1979 prison break of Assata Skakur, a revolutionary ruthlessly persecuted by the FBI in the 1960s and '70s, as well as her involvement in a 1981 Brinks robbery and a 1983 bombing of a US Senate building in response to the Reagan administration's invasion of Grenada. She received an eighty-year sentence.

I began writing Marilyn when I worked at the Beehive Collective in DC. At Beehive, we were working every day to feed people, offer free clothing and water, and we distributed pamphlets and other information about revolutionary movements around the world. We continued to decentralize decision-making, adopt new ideas about effective approaches to community work, and redefine leadership roles. This led to lively discussions with some of our neighbors who ran a Muslim bookstore.

They challenged our anarchist ideas. One of them, a former DC Black Panther, explained to me that formal leadership roles were important in their culture. For example, if they were going on a road trip to New York, they would select a "brother to be the leader of the trip," he told me. I agreed with his theorizing—his reasoning did not seem distant from our own consensus building. Trading roles was an effective way of encouraging leadership qualities; it helped avoid the scenario of a single charismatic leader being taken out, which could effectively stall a movement.

I explained to our Muslim friends that their concept of anarchy was different than ours. We were not looking to overthrow the government or participate in violence; on the contrary, we wanted to make the existing world around us a better place and participate in our community's growth. In order to do this effectively we needed to study history and approach our work in the right context. Like Marilyn, we wanted to participate; unlike Marilyn, we had her lessons to learn from. She was still behind bars and we were out in the world, at a ripe age to do our part.

Marilyn Buck's lifelong commitment to anti-racism and anti-imperialism began in the 1960s when she joined the Students for a Democratic Society at the University of Texas at Austin. She organized against the Vietnam War and helped make women's liberation a central part of SDS's politics. In the 1970s Buck worked internationally to support anti-imperialist movements around the world, while also actively supporting the Native American and black liberation movements within the US. In the early seventies she spent four years in prison for allegedly helping black revolutionaries buy firearms. When she was released, she continued her work underground. In 1973 Marilyn became a target of the FBI's COINTELPRO program, which went after members of the Black Liberation Army and the Weathermen, among others. Buck would continue to be under surveillance for the next two decades.

When the FBI captured her in San Francisco, according an unattributed pamphlet distributed on her behalf, they forced her to enter "an experimental behavior-modification program." The pamphlet goes on the point out that "the use of psychological violence and torture has been used in these prisons in order to 'neutralize' women who pose the threat of political dissidence, escape, or disruption." Like so many other US revolutionaries, Buck's experience reveals an uncomfortable truth: even before the isolation of prisoners at Guantánamo Bay, the US government was actively torturing its own citizens.

In 1979 Buck became an official suspect in Assata Shakur's successful escape from a New Jersey prison; she was captured in 1985. Meanwhile, the Black Panthers' Mutulu

Shakur (rapper Tupac Shakur's stepfather) and Sekou Odinga became suspects in the Brinks robbery in Rockland County, New York, where two police officers and a guard were shot and killed.

> With her capture in 1985, Buck became part of the Resistance Conspiracy trial. This was a prominent trial in the 1980s against seven white anti-racist and anti-imperialist activists who were accused of conspiring "to influence, change and protest policies and practices of the United States government concerning various international and domestic matters through the use of violent and illegal means." They were accused of supporting armed Black revolutionaries within the US and accused of a series of bombings of US government and military buildings in protest of US foreign policy in Central America and the Middle East. Buck received an 80-year sentence in the case.
>
> While in prison, Buck became a prolific writer of political articles and poetry. She wrote, "The trials, those years of intense repression and US government denunciations of my humanity, had beat me up rather badly. Whatever my voice had been, it was left frayed. I could scarcely speak. For prisoners, writing is a life raft to save one from drowning in a prison swamp. I could not write a diary or a journal; I was a political prisoner. Everything I had was subject to investigation, invasion and confiscation. I was a censored person. In defiance, I turned to poetry, an art of speaking sparely, but flagrantly."[133]

---

133 Staff, "US Political Prisoner Marilyn Buck Freed: Anti-Imperialist and Anti-Racist Activist Released After Decades in Prison," July 17, 2010, *Fight Back News*.

Buck faced four separate trials over the next five years, including the aforementioned Resistance Conspiracy case, which involved codefendants Laura Whitehorn, Susan Rosenberg, Linda Evans, Tim Blunk, and Dr. Alan Berkman. In 1988 Buck was sent to the women's federal maximum-security facility at Marianna, Florida. The Shawnee Unit in Marianna replaced the Lexington high-security unit after it was closed in 1988 in response to an international amnesty campaign to close the prison for its behavior-modification techniques. Buck and other political prisoners were housed in the HSU until 1994, when she was transferred to the FCI Dublin. After all her travails, she wrote, "I survived, carried on, glad to be like a weed, a wild red poppy, rooted in life."

If Marilyn Buck could survive and thrive under such conditions—even after being violently uprooted and secluded—then the work of activists at the Beehive (those seeking not to hijack a Brinks truck or bomb the Pentagon but simply to educate, inform, and mold new possibilities) needed to understand her resilience and willpower. Our work might have been daunting, but we could use her survival as our own engine of ingenuity: we needed to be like wild red poppies, undeterred.

CONFRONTING THE CONTRADICTIONS

In 1966, when the Black Power movement in the US and the Caribbean escalated and began reshaping culture, politics, and music, Haile Selassie I made his first visit to Trinidad and Tobago. Speaking to the parliament there, he pointed to a historical truth many leaders in government would do well to accept:

The systems of Government which have sought to im-

pose uniformity of belief have survived briefly and then expired, blinded and weakened by obsessive reliance upon their supposed infallibility. The only system of Government which can survive is one which is prepared to tolerate dissent and criticism and which accepts these as useful and, in any case, inevitable aspects of all social and political relations.

The tolerance of dissent and criticism within a Government proceeds from a single essential premise: that the Government exists to serve the people generally. Government servants, whether designated as representatives or not, have a trust to work for the general welfare.[134]

The Black Liberation Army was a group forced to go underground after the persecution of the Black Panther Party. While the Black Panthers confronted the status quo with fiery sociopolitical rhetoric, and advocated self-defense, contrary to their media portrayal, their stance was largely nonviolent. They instituted neighborhood services like youth breakfast programs and self-defense lessons, and protested against Republican bills like the Mumford Act, which targeted African Americans for bearing arms.

The BLA, on the other hand, engaged in their version of guerrilla warfare. Both groups stimulated disenfranchised young people to rise up against oppression, but in very different ways. As Haile Selassie I said, if governments honor dissent, that same dissent can be harnessed into a collective force for positive change. If the government had genuinely listened to the frustrations of these activist groups and worked

---

134 All Mansions of Rastafari and Culture House, *HIM 50 Jubilee Year: 1966–2016, Commemorating H.I.M. Emperor Haile Selassie I Visit to Trinidad and Tobago—April 18–21, 1966,* 2016, p. 5.

with them on even a fraction of their concerns, the effects of racial, social, and political injustice in this country might have looked very different. Instead, the US has continuously chosen to suppress dissent, persecute people desiring liberty and dignity, and broadened the rifts amongst various struggling communities.

While fervent activists, gifted orators, and committed visionaries are maligned as illegitimate by the powers that be, our government continues to respond to activism with violence. In the 1970s, after many Black Panthers were murdered, tortured, or imprisoned, the BLA adopted arms as a strategy "for the liberation and self-determination of the black people in the United States." They felt that simple self-defense wasn't adequate for their survival.

FALSE INTERNATIONALISM?
A PRINCIPLED UNITY IS OUR ONLY HOPE

Marilyn's poem talks about getting to work, joining hands, and making our dreams a reality. The question is: how can we effectively work together when we have so much pulling us apart? Race, nation, culture, gender, sexuality, sensibilities, values, tastes—these are all ways people try to divide us. How should one effectively confront the powers that be? Civil disobedience and cooperative enterprises seem to be effective methods, but even so, we still must consider the inherent power dynamics in our current social climate. The colonial mentality runs deep and its tentacles are still strangling us.

"False Internationalism," an idea put forward in the book *False Nationalism, False Internationalism,* is defined therein as "a class alliance between petty-bourgeois and lumpen opportunist elements from both oppressor and oppressed nations."[135] In this theory, oppressor nations retain control over others through internal agents. *False Nationalism, False Internationalism* also outlines the parasitic relationship between black and white revolutionaries: "Correct relations between revolutionaries of different nations must be based on the principle of equality and mutual respect; this means respect for the right of self-determination of the oppressed nations in all matters."[136] It was Black Panther Fred Hampton who famously said in 1968, "We've got to face the fact that some people say you fight fire best with fire, but we say you put fire out best with water. We say you don't fight racism with racism. We're gonna fight racism with solidarity."[137]

For this reason, I appreciated when Dhoruba Bin Wahad pointed to a "principled unity" as our primary hope in 1995, when I saw him speak at a press conference in Philadelphia for the tenth anniversary of the MOVE house bombing: "Unity with others must be based on common principles and their adherence must be taken seriously." The press conference included MOVE members, testimonies from eyewitnesses, and words from Giancarlo Esposito, who starred in Spike Lee's movie *Do the Right Thing* and more recently the AMC series *Breaking Bad*.

As much as Rastafari has fueled my activism, the MOVE organization has also offered me tremendous inspiration. In my mind, MOVE is like a homegrown version of Rastafari; many points in their ideologies seem to converge. All members took the surname "Africa" regardless of their race; they

---

135 Assata Shakur, Mumia Abu-Jamal, and Dhoruba Bin Wahad, *Still Black, Still Strong: Survivors of the War Against Black Revolutionaries* (Semiotext(e), 1993), p. 3–4.

136 E. Tani and Kaé Sera, *False Nationalism, False Internationalism: Class Contradictions in the Armed Struggle* (A Seeds Beneath the Snow Publication, 1985), p. 27.

137 Amy Sonnie and James Tracy, *Hillbilly Nationalists, Urban Race Rebels, and Black Power* (Melville House, 2011), p. 66.

collectively acknowledged that all of humanity originated in Africa.

Racism was a vital element in demonizing prominent MOVE members. When I was growing up in DC, a predominantly black city, racism was a preoccupation in my daily life. I was called "white boy," "nigger," "miscegenated," "African-looking motherfucker," and more. I've defended myself from every side of the aisle, and I ultimately found a tenuously comfortable place in between. It was a powerful moment when I learned that Bob Marley felt similarly about his own place in society. In fact, when I was in high school, I wore a pin on my jacket of Marley's face and many people thought it was me. Previously I wasn't sure whom I looked like. Sure, I resembled my siblings, but I was the brownest child and this in its own way shaped my life in this racially complex world.

RACE?

Different ethnicities have been mixing since ancient times (as popular DNA tests verify), so no lineage consists solely of only one *race*. Ancient Rome, for example, was as diverse as contemporary New York City.

J.A. Rogers, an early-twentieth-century Jamaican-American journalist, publisher, historian, and Pullman porter, penned many books that became fixtures in Afrocentric bookstores around the US, including pamphlets like *From "Superman" to Man*, self-published in 1917, *As Nature Leads: An Informal Discussion of the Reason Why Negro and Caucasian are Mixing in Spite of Opposition*, and *The Thrilling Story of the Maroons*. *The Real Facts About Ethiopia*, his 1936 book featuring the likeness of Haile Selassie I on the front, developed a Rasta cult following. But one of Rogers's later books,

Nature Knows No Color-Line: Research into the Negro Ancestry in the White Race, remains his seminal work, for he writes a dazzling account that thoroughly and historically discredits race as a distinct human category. In Rogers's prose, race is understood as a modern social construction:

> *Race, as we now use it, [French anthropologist Topinard] says, was unknown in far antiquity, at least in the West. He correctly notes that Aristotle, Father of Natural History, and Hippocrates, Father of Medicine, do not even mention "race" though both studied anatomy and the then known varieties of the human race, including the Negro.*
>
> *The Greek had two distinct divisions of humanity— Greek and Barbarian, or citizen and alien. An Athenian who married an alien, regardless of color, was sold into slavery. It was for a long time the same in Rome. "Race" as based on color and physique is, in fact, comparatively recent. The King James Bible of the seventeenth century does not mention it. Shakespeare used it only for family lineage or contests. So also do the first English dictionary by Nathaniel Bailey in 1736; and the second by Dr. Samuel Johnson in 1750.[138]*

As MOVE pointed out, human beings all come from an original root. Thus, people's physiology, no matter their "race," remains mostly the same. On this subject Haile Selassie I was very clear—in an interview on *Meet the Press* in October 1963, he said that "black and white, as forms of speech, and as a means of judging mankind, should be eliminated

---

138 J.A. Rogers, *Nature Knows No Color-Line* (Helga M. Rogers, 1980), p. 10.

from human society. Human beings are precisely the same whatever color, race, creed or national origin they may be."

In contemporary society, race is a by-product of European colonialism and the institution of slavery, which demonizes otherness and difference. Such social conditioning has a permanent, lasting effect, including the monitoring, profiling, and overpolicing of minority communities today, which result in the skewed makeup of the domestic prison population. For example, in 2016, black people were 5.1 times more likely to be incarcerated than whites, though African Americans only comprise 13.3 percent of the nation's overall population.

No matter how color-blind one tries to be, the social and historical realities prove that race matters, and people's experiences differ because of it. This manifests in sometimes very confusing and subtle forms of privilege and deprivation. The book *Racecraft* by Karen and Barbara Fields likens the concept of race to witchcraft; it's not real, but because people think it is, it has very real consequences.

In *The Invention of the White Race*, Theodore Allen argues that this social contract has a purpose. It "meant not only that no Euro-Americans were slaves, but also that all Euro-Americans, even laborers, were by definition enforcers of slavery."[139] To ignore this reality, an absolutely monumental social dynamic in America, and pretend that a black president validates a color-blind society, is a mistake. Barack Obama's presidency witnessed an unsettling upsurge of racism-related incidents. In 2015, hate crimes against Muslims rose 67 percent, and hate crimes across all categories

---

139 Noel Ignatiev, "Treason to Whiteness Is Loyalty to Humanity: An Interview with Noel Ignatiev of *Race Traitor* Magazine," excerpted from the anarchist tabloid *THE BLAST!* (June/July 1994), p. 177.

peaked after the election of Donald Trump. America, it seems, is by no means color-blind. It is color-divided.

In 1965, just before the formation of the Black Panthers, Selassie I discussed the ramification of race conflict on world peace. "The untenable doctrine of racial supremacy," he said, is a "threat to the maintenance of international peace and security as well as a serious set-back for establishing a salubrious atmosphere of understanding and co-operation in the world, [and so] we must work together against the philosophy of racism."[140]

In America, such a pronounced divide in the perception of races was not always the norm, as Bacon's Rebellion highlights:

In the Chesapeake Bay Colony (Virginia and Maryland), people from Africa and people from Europe worked together in the tobacco fields. They mated with each other, ran away and rebelled together, at first. At the end of the 1600s, people of African descent, even those who were free, lost certain rights they had before and that even the poorest and most downtrodden person of European descent continued to enjoy. In return for these privileges, European-Americans of all classes came to be part of the apparatus that maintained Afro-Americans in chattel slavery (and themselves in unfreedom). That was the birth of "race." As we use the term.[141]

In *The New Jim Crow*, Michelle Alexander details the

140 Haile Selassie I, *Selected Speeches of His Imperial Majesty Haile Selassie I* (One Drop Books, 2000), p. 381.

141 Noel Ignatiev, "Treason to Whiteness Is Loyalty to Humanity: An Interview with Noel Ignatiev of *Race Traitor* Magazine," excerpted from the *THE BLAST!* (June/July 1994), p. 177.

racial caste system in America, first in slavery and then in the form of Jim Crow laws. As she explains, the lawful supression of black people was later redesigned as the "War on Drugs," which now shapes the current prison-industrial complex. Alexander details some of the early strategies implemented in order to imprison black people:

> *Deliberately and strategically, the planter class extended special privileges to poor whites in an effort to drive a wedge between them and black slaves. White settlers were allowed greater access to Native American lands, white servants were allowed to police slaves through slave patrols and militias, and barriers were created so that free labor would not be placed in competition with slave labor. These measures effectively eliminated the risk of future alliances between black slaves and poor whites. Poor whites suddenly had a direct, personal stake in the existence of a race-based system of slavery. Their own plight had not improved by much, but at least they were not slaves. Once the planter elite split the labor force, poor whites responded to the logic of their situation and sought ways to expand their racially privileged position.* [142]

Noel Ignatiev, former Communist, steel mill worker, organizer, Harvard-trained academic, and cofounder and co-editor of the journal *Race Traitor* and the *New Abolitionist Society*, boldly proclaims that "treason to whiteness is loyalty to humanity." His perspective suggests the "white race" can undo its own paradigm of power. "Many black people have European ancestors and plenty so-called whites have African

---

142 Michelle Alexander, *The New Jim Crow: Mass Incarceration in the Age of Color-blindness* (The New Press, 2010), p. 25

or Native American ancestors," he says. "No biologist has ever been able to provide a satisfactory definition of race . . . Attempts to do so lead to absurdities: mothers and children of different races, or the phenomenon that a white woman can give birth to a black child, but a black woman can never give birth to a white child." Ignatiev furthers reflects upon "the only possible conclusion . . . people are members of different races because they are assigned to them."[143]

For social, political, and cultural change to occur, actions must be taken. Whiteness has to be *abolished* so the system can correct itself and expunge white privilege. Ignatiev believes "black" and "white" are categories made and maintained, not inherently natural, hence they act as "political categories." Whiteness, simply put, is the willingness to seek a comfortable place within the system of race privilege. "While not all forms of injustice can be collapsed into whiteness," Ignatiev states, "undermining white race solidarity opens the door to fundamental social change in other areas."[144] Jesse McDade argues in *Frantz Fanon: The Ethical Justification of Revolution* that Fanon makes it clear in *Black Skin, White Masks* that being labeled white or black creates cleavages between people. McDade writes, "The Negro and the white man must turn their backs upon the divisive categories of black and white and look inward for that universal characteristic which makes total personhood possible."[145] And here's what Fanon says in his conclusion: "Both must turn their backs on the inhuman voices which were those of their respective ancestors in order that authentic communication be possible. Before

143   Noel Ignatiev, "Treason to Whiteness Is Loyalty to Humanity: An Interview with Noel Ignatiev of *Race Traitor* Magazine," excerpted from *THE BLAST!* (June/July 1994), p. 177.

144   *Ibid*, p. 178.

145   Jesse N. McDade, *Frantz Fanon: The Ethical Justification of Revolution* (Boston University, 1970), p. 60.

it can adopt a positive voice, freedom requires an effort at disalienation."[146]

Both the Beehive Collective and the politically charged songs I wrote were attempts to fissure, undermine, and subvert whiteness—to collapse the façade and create seeds of change. Some thought our organization existed in a cocoon; in reality we were Trojan horses ready to remake culture from within. When my first band Soulside did a cross-country reunion tour in 2016, playing thirty-year-old songs with lyrics that easily applied to the current context, it couldn't have been more clear that the threat of an expanding racial divide is only more real today.

SETBACKS IN THE MOVEMENT

The early 1980s saw the political defeat of many sixties activists. After the Weather Underground, Marilyn Buck became active with the Revolutionary Armed Task Force, described as a "Black/white alliance under New Afrikan leadership." Although they carried out a series of successful bank robberies, the authors of *False Nationalism, False Internationalism* write,

> *RATF was totally out-planned and out-maneuvered by the State security forces, despite the courage and fighting ability of individual RATF fighters. The FBI had a superior grasp of strategic political-military factors, and was playing a deeper political game. Which was how they could not only wipe RATF out militarily, but also inflict a stinging political defeat.*[147]

---

146 Frantz Fanon, *Black Skin, White Masks* (Grove Press, 2008), p. 180.

147 E. Tani and Kaé Sera, *False Nationalism, False Internationalism: Class Contradictions in the Armed Struggle* (A Seeds Beneath the Snow Publication, 1985), p. 240.

Members of RATF were maligned in the media, leading them to be characterized as common criminals; even the
book I have been citing, *False Nationalism, False Internationalism*, criticizes them, stating that their legacy was to "degrade
the revolution of its moral superiority, its integrity in the eyes
of the masses . . . FBI exposure of the moral corruption
within RATF was perhaps the most damaging political blow.
It was a propaganda coup to be able to smear the New Afrikan Independence Movement and the BLA as being associated with cowards, traitors, confused people, drug dealing,
and pimping."[148]

Victories against colonial powers succeed when rebellion
forces work in harmony despite differences. Martin Luther
King Jr. and the Civil Rights Movement succeeded because
they put pressure on presiding power structures. If legal institutions had not engaged King, they would have had to deal
with Malcolm X and the Black Power movement, of whom
they were deeply afraid.

I was in my early twenties when my friends and I opened
the Beehive, which we later found out was blocks away from
the DC Black Panther headquarters. As a punk participant, I
knew the Beehive should engage the progressive institutions
across the city, from food pantries and health clinics, to ten-
ants' rights groups and centers for abused children.

We started an Anarchist Black Cross chapter because we
wanted to raise awareness about the dramatically expanding
prison-industrial complex. Mumia Abu-Jamal and Leonard
Peltier were high-profile political prisoners, but many other
revolutionaries from the sixties and seventies also languished

---

148 *Ibid*, p. 240.

behind bars, silenced by the state. As a collective, we studied a variety of books by and about revolutionaries; we were very interested in looking at their successes and failures, so that we could forge our own path forward. Emma Goldman and Antonio Gramsci were inspirations for us, as were Butch Lee and Red Rover.

To help amplify these marginalized voices, we arranged a variety of speaking engagements at DC libraries. Lorenzo "Komboa" Ervin, from the Chattanooga Black Panther Party and author of *Anarchism and the Black Revolution*, and Ramona Africa from MOVE were two of our first speaking guests. We were able to spend significant time with both of them, gaining insight into their experiences and how they saw the movement continuing. Given what Ramona had been through in Philadelphia, she was an especially inspiring character.

Motivated by my interactions with these activists, I wrote Marilyn Buck. She is readily criticized in *False Nationalism, False Internationalism*, and I wanted to clarify these critiques with her. I sent her an early copy of this book, *Revolutionary Threads*, so she could understand my context for writing her. Here's one of her responses:

> Greetings Bobby,
>   . . . You asked about <u>False Nationalism.</u> I hated it when it came out because it was strident and attacking, lacking in comradely style criticism. I likely agree with some of the criticisms, but at a period when under attack by the State it was hard to deal with or respond to. The folks who wrote it? Yes I knew them—friends who had differences and left. In later life one learns that perhaps we should have known how to listen better—set aside who's correct.

Did you finish the book or put poem to music? Or did my silence, silence your wish? If so I'm sorry. I didn't feel able to really give a perspective on False Nationalism, False Internationalism. At this point, not having read the book for twenty years, I'm a bit bummed out with the prison world and daily repression. As to my poem, I hope you did set it to music. Just give me credit. Send a copy of the CD to my friends to hear. I can't get anything like that. If I do find your manuscript do you still want comments? Thank you for your interest and again, I'm sorry to have been such a foot dragger. So write again if you like.

Sincerely,
Marilyn Buck

We exchanged many more letters over the years and she requested I change a few words in her poem to match the modern moment. For example, one line was written originally as: "Hoes, hammers, hand grenades and other hands . . ." She asked me to remove "hand grenades," mentioning that she was trying to get out of prison and didn't want anything to keep that from happening. Her strategy had changed over the years and she wanted the poem to reflect her present thinking. When I sent my song to her friends, they reported positively back to her. She also read the entire manuscript I sent her, discussed Rastafari sistren and brethren behind bars, and thanked me for my information and insight.

Perspectives from incarcerated people like Buck are often valuable. Their daily lives are the result of repressive government policy—twenty-four hours a day, seven days a week. The behavior of the prison administrations at Guantánamo

Bay, Abu Ghraib, and various other sites around the world are an extension of the brutal, long-standing, and often hidden policies enacted upon activists throughout our nation's history.

Marilyn Buck's dreams are familiar to many who live outside prison walls. She did not rise from "clear blue days" because she was writing from within the "dark cells" of one of America's gulags. But her dreams are like many peoples' dreams. Many of us are compelled to find ways to work together to stoke the "Flame of Liberation" within our hearts and manifest a world that must not continue to systematically demean, exploit, and subjugate its people and their natural resources.

CHAPTER 6

SEVENTIES HEROES

Assata and Zayd Shakur, I wonder if they knew for sure,
This would be the last day that they would spend together.
They went for a drive on the Jersey Turnpike,
Shots rang out and got Zayd, much to the policeman's
pleasure.

Assata was wounded for sure, they beat her behind a
prison door,
But the walls could not hold her; her friends broke in
and she escaped.
Sundiata got away, he was driving with them that day,
But they caught him after three days; he's been in prison
since '73.

So who were the real American heroes? In the seventies
it wasn't Nixon or Spiro.
Could it have been the revolutionaries working under-
ground to keep the people free?
So who were the real American heroes? In the seventies
it wasn't Ribner or Rizzo.
Could it have been John Africa's revolution, the Seed of
Wisdom, the fight against pollution?

There's so many people struggling,
There's so many people hustling,
There's a new generation coming in
And we need the light they're bringing.

Imam Al-Amin, Dhoruba Bin Wahad, George and Jon-
athan Jackson,

After Al-Hajj Malik El-Shabazz,
Geronimo Pratt, Sekou Odinga, and Herman Bell,
Mutulu and Kuwasi Balagoon, Sha Sha, Blood, Jalil,
and Nuh Washington.

Revolutionaries in the US have more in common with Rastas than just dreadlocks. They grapple with sociopolitical undercurrents, varied and even sectarian beliefs, and issues surrounding community involvement. Horace Campbell, whose pivotal work *Rasta and Resistance* is a prominent study in Rastafari's relationship with revolution, profoundly points out, "Rastafari faith, or even early liberation theology, has not escaped the dilemma which each of the great religions, especially Hinduism and Christianity, has set itself—the conflict between faith and works, contemplation and action." He continues: "The fact that this very conflict now grips the soul of Rastafari, in relation to politics, is not a sign of collapse but of maturity. So it is that there are differences of opinion among the Rasta, whether it is their work to storm the earthly kingdom and take it in order to change it; or to explain it, to enquire more deeply into the Maker and His mysteries; or to engage in both warfares."[149]

This chapter is about some of those who engaged.

A BLOODY DECADE FOR REVOLUTIONARIES IN THE USA

Although 1970s America is culturally associated with the decadence of disco and the end of the idealistic sixties, it was also a time when revolutionary and reactionary forces went underground to forward their struggles outside of governmental view. It was a difficult time for revolutionaries in-

---

149 Horace Campbell, *Rasta and Resistance: From Marcus Garvey to Walter Rodney* (Africa World Press, 1987), p. x.

volved in the Black Power and Civil Rights movements; the new decade began with strikingly significant flash points.

On August 7, 1970, Black Panther Jonathan Jackson was slain in the Marion County courthouse in Indianapolis, during an attempt to free his older brother, George Jackson. Behind bars, George Jackson helped form the Black Guerrilla Family and later became the subject of Bob Dylan and Steel Pulse songs. He was also the author of the best-selling book *Soledad Brother*. Both brothers were quite famous at the time, and the book was largely a collection of letters between them.

In the courthouse that day, Jonathan tried to free George and the other Soledad Brothers through the kidnapping of Supreme Court judge Harold Haley. Jonathan was killed on site, but his actions prompted the hunt and capture of another outspoken critic of the American judicial system: Angela Davis, a professor at the University of California, San Diego. The firearms Jonathan used in the courthouse were registered under her name; he had been one of her bodyguards. Jonathan's courthouse incident spun out of control as multiple hostages were taken and there was a shootout between the police and the escaping van. In addition to Jonathan, three other people were killed that day—two of Jonathan's accomplices and the judge. Several more hostages were wounded by the gunfire.

Perhaps in retaliation for his brother's actions, a prison guard shot and killed George Jackson in the back on August 21, 1971. The prison said George was attempting to escape, but many activists viewed it as a deliberate assassination. Less than a month later, on September 13, 1971, the single bloodiest day in US prison history occurred: after a botched raid to suppress a thousand inmates who had revolted and seized

sections of the Attica Correctional Facility, thirty-three prisoners were massacred and ten corrections officers and em-
ployees were killed. The inmates stood their ground against
the guards for five days, seeking to negotiate an end to their
inhumane conditions as well as protest George Jackson's
murder. "We are men! We are not beasts," they are reported
as chanting. Despite racial conflict, Attica prisoners fought
across the color line for a common cause—the majority of
the inmates were African American, but there was a sub-
stantial Puerto Rican population. The 383 correctional officers, however, were white. As reported, many of the guards
were openly racist and apparently called their batons "nigger
sticks."

The government feared George Jackson because of his
incredible leadership potential and formidable determina-
tion. Due the success of *Soledad Brother*, Jackson's voice in-
vigorated many people with a sense of urgency. In the text,
after discussing the brutal killings behind prison walls, he
proclaims, "Our mortality rate is almost what you expect to
find in a history of Dachau."

At the age of eighteen, Jackson had been sentenced one
year to life for a seventy-dollar armed robbery. In prison, he
became politicized and an outspoken critic of the American
government. His activism essentially guaranteed a lifetime
sentence. In 1966 inside San Quentin Prison, Jackson and
other prisoners started the aforementioned Black Guerrilla
Family. It was an organization set up to defend the rights of
black inmates. Danny Haiphong, a writer for the *Black Agenda
Report*, explains, "George Jackson was a giant that the US
State could not contain—so it killed him. It was Jackson
who developed a foundational theory of the prison state in
relationship to the design of the imperialist system. Jackson

said revolutionary movements require three elements: 'an above-ground organization that carries out political work, an independent media, and an underground organization committed to creating crises for the establishment.'"[150]

Jackson's political positions were shaped by his firsthand experience. He advocated for worldwide revolution and was not rebellious with a criminal's intent. As Eric Mann argues, "George doesn't use fascism as an angry curse at the rulers. He presents it as an analytical model to explain the nature of US society that can help us better understand the nature of our enemy and work out the most effective strategies for resistance."[151]

More than thirty years have passed since George Jackson's murder, but law enforcement officials still operate with animosity toward revolutionaries. A prominent example of this came in 2005, when Tookie Williams's stay of execution was denied by California governor Arnold Schwarzenegger, in part because Tookie cited George Jackson as one of his heroes. Tookie was a prominent Los Angeles gang member who evolved into a positive role model for young inmates in prison; he taught others to serve their sentences without inciting or encouraging violent incidents. Despite Tookie's exemplary conduct in prison for more than a decade, the state still executed him. He was even nominated for a Nobel Peace Prize after he worked on a peace accord between rival LA gangs and publicly lamented his role in forming the Cripps. Despite such deeds, Schwarzenegger denied Williams clemency. In his statement, the governnor said: "The dedication

---

150   Danny Haiphong, "Why George Jackson Matters Through the Lens of *Blood in My Eye*," *Black Agenda Report*, September 9, 2015.

151   Eric Mann, *Comrade George: An Investigation into the Life, Political Thought, and Assassination of George Jackson* (Harper and Row, 1974), p. 161.

of Williams's book *Life in Prison* cast significant doubt on his personal redemption. . . The mix of individuals on [the dedication] list is curious . . . But the inclusion of George Jackson on the list defies reason and is a significant indicator that Williams is not reformed . . ."[152]

In 1970, activist H. Rap Brown was charged with inciting to riot in Cambridge, Maryland, and was placed on the FBI's Most Wanted list. At only twenty-three years of age, he was the chairman of the Student Nonviolent Coordinating Committee and a strong member of the Civil Rights Movement; Brown worked tirelessly registering black voters in the South and later became minister of justice for the Black Panther Party.

In 1971, the FBI captured Brown in New York City and sent him to Attica prison on a robbery conviction. After five years of incarceration, he emerged from prison as Jamil Al-Amin, a devout Muslim. He made a pilgrimage to Mecca and then settled in a neighborhood in Atlanta's West End, where he became active in the Muslim community. In 2002, journalist Mara Shalhoup wrote:

> *Today, West End Park is lined by manicured yards and white-trimmed bungalows painted lemon yellow, teal and taupe. Boys shoot hoops on a covered basketball court, and women in bright headscarves gather on the lawn across the street. All signs point toward prosperity.*
>
> *It was a different scene in the late 1970s and early 1980s. Those gathered in the park were not there for play but to sell services and wares: sex, and later, crack rock.*
>
> *Within a decade the drugs and prostitutes began to*

---

152   Dave Zirin, "Why Arnold Killed Tookie," *Alternet* (December 13, 2005).

disappear. Al-Amin's followers like to credit him with the street sweeping, but no one can say for sure that he was creating the resurgence of West End. He did join the local mosque and become its prayer leader. Muslim families from Boston, Philadelphia and New York relocated to West End to be closer to the mosque and its charismatic leader.

"We developed West End at the height of the crack epidemic, enforced the park's curfew to keep out the bad elements," says Ali, now heading the West End mosque in Al-Amin's absence. "We cleaned it up by having a visible presence of [Muslim] men in this neighborhood."[153]

After Jamil Al-Amin was released from prison, the police tracked him incessantly. In 1993, he was interrogated as a suspect in the first World Trade Center bombing. A year later, he was charged with shooting a man in the leg outside of the store he owned. Later, the victim accused the police of provoking Al-Amin into shooting him. The charges were dropped, and the victim joined Al-Amin's mosque in the West End. But immediately after they arrested Al-Amin for the bogus shooting, FBI agents invaded his store. (This incident occurred only one month after NYPD officers were acquitted for the brutal slaying of Amadou Diallo, an unarmed twenty-three-year-old immigrant from Guinea. Diallo was a devout Muslim and a law-abiding citizen. Police fired over forty shots into him as he stood in the foyer of his apartment building.)

Deputies Aldranon English and Ricky Kinchen, who ironically also served the warrant to Al-Amin, had both been

---

153 Mara Shalhoup, "As American As Cherry Pie," *Creative Loafing Atlanta* (January 23, 2002).

on the force for less than a year. Heavily armed and inexperienced, their first approach to his store was fruitless; the second time it was lethal.

Al-Amin was thought to have killed Kinchen and wounded English. When he was finally apprehended, though, the case against him was very thin. Nonetheless, at the time of this writing, Al-Amin remains in prison enduring inhumane conditions, including solitary confinement and restricted access to his Quran.

THE CARIBBEAN CONNECTION

Walter Rodney was a noted historian and political figure in the 1960s and '70s; he released his best-known book, *How Europe Underdeveloped Africa*, in 1972. In 1966, when Rodney was just twenty-four, he was awarded a PhD with honors in African history from the School of Oriental and African Studies in London. His dissertation, "A History of the Upper Guinea Coast, 1545–1800," was published in 1970. A devoted student of C.L.R. James, Rodney became a professor of African history at the University of the West Indies in Jamaica, where he was introduced to the burgeoning culture of Rastafari. He instructed his classes in both a formal university setting and in remote regions of Jamaica's countryside via "groundings" with Rastafari sistren and brethren. The reasoning sessions he facilitated are recorded in *Groundings with My Brothers*—his mission was to debunk any uneducated glorification of the African past by teaching a true history of the African continent. Originally born in Guyana, Rodney was assassinated in his home country after returning from an independence celebration in Zimbabwe. Authorities deplored Rodney's revolutionary zeal; he expertly voiced the people's dire need for change.

The revolutionary vigor in America in the 1960s and '70s was part of a global phenomenon, and our close Caribbean neighbors were no exception. In Grenada, Rastas mobilized to take part in the revolution. According to Horace Campbell, "More than 400 Rastas were involved in the People's Liberation Army, which overthrew the Eric Gairy dictatorship on 13 March, 1979."[154] The New Jewel Movement championed the Rastas against ganja charges, placing them in "key governmental positions in the security forces" and proclaiming, "Rastafari must take their proper place in the Third World Revolution struggle against dictatorship and oppression. Rastas cannot and must not become the pawns of reactionary capitalists in their attempt to maintain imperialism."[155] There was clearly an interchange going on throughout the region, and the successful revolution in Cuba was a beacon.

In 2016, I traveled to Cuba with the National Cooperative Business Association. Our delegation engaged Cuba's cooperative sector in as many ways as we could. Since the US embargo was still effectively in place, we hoped to pave the way for future co-op collaborations. I was working with the NCBA CLUSA's US-Cuba Cooperative Working Group, along with others from True Value Hardware, Organic Valley, the US Federation of Worker Cooperatives, and more. I was excited to do some work with the co-ops in Cuba, but what would have made the trip even more special would have been to link up with an idol of mine, Assata Shakur.

---

154 Horace Campbell, *Rasta and Resistance: From Marcus Garvey to Walter Rodney* (Africa World Press, 1987), p. 163.

155 *Ibid*, p. 173.

ASSATA SHAKUR AND THE BLACK LIBERATION ARMY

At the end of the 1960s, the Black Panther Party began to split. After merciless persecution, different perspectives clashed: some members wanted guerrilla warfare, others wanted a nonviolent political movement. Geronimo Pratt had gone underground to work on an independent "New African" Southern state. Apparently, this caused his removal from the BPP. After the Panther 21 made a statement supporting the Weather Underground, they too were removed.

The Panther 21 was a group of New York Black Panthers arrested and charged in April 1969 for conspiracy to blow up the New York Botanical Gardens; the jury acquitted them after just forty-five minutes of deliberation. Afeni Shakur (Tupac's mother), Dhoruba Bin Wahad, Jamal Joseph, Kwando Kinshasa, Shaba Om, Ali Bey Hassan, Curtis Powell, Richard Harris, and Kuwasi Balagoon were all involved.

The FBI's ruthless persecution of the Black Panther Party forced many members into hiding. This gave rise to the Black Liberation Army, a self-proclaimed "New African guerrilla organization." The song lyrics that preface this chapter refer to a 1973 incident involving BLA members Sundiata Acoli, Assata Shakur, and Zayd Malik Shakur. State troopers ambushed them while they were driving on the New Jersey Turnpike and ultimately Zayd was killed and Assata was shot twice. Assata later stated:

> I was kept on the floor, kicked, pulled, dragged along by my hair. Finally I was put into an ambulance, but the police would not let the ambulance leave. They kept asking the ambulance attendant: "Is she dead yet? Is she dead yet?" Finally when it was clear I wasn't going to die in the next five or ten minutes, they took me to the hospital.

The police were jumping on me, beating me, choking me,
doing everything they could possibly do as soon as the
doctors or the nurses would go outside.[156]

On November 2, 1979, the Revolutionary Armed Task
Force liberated Assata Shakur from prison and whisked her
away to safety in Cuba. Assata apparently still resides there
today, safe and sound, albeit with million-dollar bounty on
her head, courtesy of the George W. Bush administration.

THE MOVE ORGANIZATION

The MOVE organization emerged in Philadelphia in the sev-
enties. Like the movement of Rastafari, their focus on stop-
ping pollution and animal cruelty was dramatically ahead
of its time. In their self-published booklet *20 Years on the
MOVE*, they defiantly stated in capital letters: "MOVE'S
WORK IS TO STOP INDUSTRY FROM POISONING
THE AIR, THE WATER, THE SOIL, AND TO PUT AN
END TO THE ENSLAVEMENT OF LIFE—PEOPLE, AN-
IMALS, ANY FORM OF LIFE."

MOVE had a very innovative approach to resisting
the criminal justice system. When members started getting
locked up on a regular basis, they used "strategic profanity," as they called it. Their logic was that words were not
profane, only the system that oppressed others was profane.
They also strategically decided who would get arrested at
each protest. Then at the hearings they would have ten or
so members disrupt the trial. This meant that the case would
get suspended and ten more people would be charged with
contempt. MOVE members did this over and over until city

---

156 Assata Shakur, Mumia Abu-Jamal, and Dhoruba Bin Wahad, *Still Black, Still
Strong: Survivors of the War Against Black Revolutionaries* (Semiotext(e), 1993), p. 205.

officials were forced to drop the cases against them; the system could not manage the workload.

MOVE members ate a plant-based diet and embraced hard physical work. Living as a family, they adopted homeschooling as their primary means for educating their youth. They chopped their own firewood, ran dogs, shoveled snow, and swept the street. They helped homeless people find shelter and assisted the elderly with home repairs. Well-known political prisoner Mumia Abu-Jamal was a local journalist at the time of MOVE's emergence, and he describes his relationship with them this way:

> I met MOVE while covering them in Philadelphia. No one who was in Philadelphia from the seventies to the mid-eighties can claim not to know about MOVE. MOVE members have been active and aboveground in Philadelphia since 1973. I've been reading in magazines a lot about the animal liberation movement. In 1973 they were in the Philadelphia Zoo protesting caged exploitation of animals, and they were beaten for it, they were jailed for it, and they got ridiculously high bails for it. When I first heard about MOVE people eating garlic, the women having babies with no midwife, no drugs, no medication, no husband, just themselves and their God-given instinct for motherhood . . . about MOVE people being beaten for protesting Frank Rizzo or protesting at the zoo against the encagement of animals, I thought they were crazy . . . What MOVE represents is an idea that people can move away from the system and use the principle of life to survive . . . There's nothing more powerful than an idea.[157]

---

157 Assata Shakur, Mumia Abu-Jamal, and Dhoruba Bin Wahad, *Still Black, Still Strong: Survivors of the War Against Black Revolutionaries* (Semiotext(e), 1993), pgs.

MOVE's striking radicalism ramped up when a police of-ficer trampled one of their newborn babies to death. The cir-cumstance of the baby's murder prompted MOVE to host a press conference. Needless to say, the police department, run by the notorious Frank Rizzo, was not congenial. In 1978, two years after this tragic incident, the police carried out a full-on siege of a MOVE house following a housing code vi-olation, going as far as using water cannons and firepower. Consuewella and Janet Africa carried children out of the flooded basement and Delbert Africa was savagely beaten on international television.

Nine MOVE members were eventually convicted for the killing of a police officer. He was shot at a downward tra-jectory in the back of the neck while the MOVE members were confined to the basement of their house. The angle of the shot points conclusively to "friendly fire," but this is very rarely, if ever, reported in the media. The judge in the case made the startling admission "that he 'hadn't the faintest idea' who really fired the fatal shot. 'They call themselves a family,' the judge said. 'I'll sentence them as a family."[158] Those nine MOVE members are still incarcerated at the time of this writing—almost four decades later!

MOVE was reborn in the eighties at a row house in West Philly, where they broadcasted their strategic profanity from a loudspeaker; they set it up one Christmas Eve and screamed about how much of a "motherfucker" Santa Claus was. The mayor and the police commissioner classified them as a terrorist organization, although the revamped MOVE

117–119.

158 Terry Bisson, On a Move: The Story of Mumia Abu-Jamal (Litmus Books, 2000), p. 170.

house had yet to commit a violent act. Their weapons were words, and they faced a foe that was ready to use explosives. On May 13, 1985, MOVE's row house was bombed, resulting in the death of five children and six adults. Ramona Africa and thirteen-year-old Birdy Africa were the only ones to survive the attack. As the only adult survivor, Ramona was later incarcerated for rioting and conspiracy.

In 1996, after regularly traveling to Philadelphia with the Beehive and taking part in Mumia demonstrations, I visited the Philadelphia courthouse holding MOVE's civil suit against the city. We watched as the judge ordered the city to pay $1.5 million to Ramona and various relatives of others killed in the incident. The MOVE members defied expectations. These are passionate people who want to be heard, but are also willing to listen. The MOVE organization taught its members to be leaders and prepared them for legal persecution and a lifetime of struggle. When pressed by the authorities, they practiced courtroom techniques which were very effective.

"We didn't start out confronting the court system and going into court," Ramona Africa said in a 1996 interview. "We were having peaceful demonstrations at the Philadelphia Zoo, at unsafe boarding homes for the elderly, the board of education, and the police started coming at us and attacking us, to stop our demonstrations."[159] That's when they developed the tactic of clogging the courts with their cases.

MOVE's tactics might seem intense and occasionally brash, but in light of today's worldwide consciousness of climate change and police brutality, John Africa's teachings might have made positive strides toward correcting these

---

159 Pedro Sanchez, "Interview with Ramona Africa," *Prison News Service* #55, October 1996.

atrocities. Here's more of the pivotal perspective MOVE offered:

OUR RELIGION—LIFE

JOHN AFRICA taught us that Life is the priority. Nothing is more important or as important as Life, the force that keeps us alive. All life comes from one source, from God, Mom Nature, Mama. Each individual life is dependent on every other life, and all life has a purpose, so all living beings, things that move, are equally important, whether they are human beings, dogs, birds, fish, trees, ants, weeds, rivers, wind, or rain. To stay healthy and strong, life must have clean air, clear water, and pure food. If deprived of these things, life will cycle to the next level, or as the system says, "die."

NATURAL LAW

We believe in natural law, the government of self. Man-made laws are not really laws, because they don't apply equally to everyone and they contain exceptions and loopholes. Man-made laws are constantly being amended or repealed. Natural law stays the same and always has. Man's laws require police, sheriffs, armies, and courts to enforce them, and lawyers to explain them. True law is self-explanatory and self-enforcing. In the undisturbed jungles, oceans, deserts of the world, there are no courtrooms or jails. The animals and plants don't need them. No living being has to consult a law book to be able to know if they have to cough, sneeze, or urinate. Natural law says that when you see something getting too close to your eye, you will blink, whether you are a German shepherd or a Supreme Court Justice.

SELF-DEFENSE

All living things instinctively defend themselves. This is a God-given right of all life. If a man goes into a bear's cave, he violates and threatens the bear's place of security. The bear will defend his home by instinctively fighting off the man and eliminating him. The bear is not wrong, because self-defense is right.

BEING A REVOLUTIONARY

Revolution starts with the individual. It starts with a person making a personal commitment to do what's right. You can't turn someone into a revolutionary by making them chant slogans or wave guns. To understand revolution, you must be sound. Revolution is not imposed upon another, it is kindled within them. A person can talk about revolution, but if they are still worshipping money, or putting drugs into their body, or beating their mate, they obviously haven't committed themselves to doing what's right. Revolution is not a philosophy, it is an activity.[160]

1974—THE OVERTHROW OF SELASSIE I

America and the Caribbean weren't the only places bursting with revolutionary fervor. In the seventies, Ethiopian citizens were frustrated with the emperor; they wanted further progress. What many didn't see was that Haile Selassie I was making the strides they were looking for, and due to Rastas, history remains on his side. "If the revolution is good for the people, then I am for the revolution," Selassie I said.[161]

---

160 *20 Years on the MOVE* (1993), pgs. 68–69. Reprinted here with permission. An updated version can be found at www.onamove.com.

161 Ryszard Kapuściński, *The Emperor: Downfall of an Autocrat* (Vintage Books

In prior decades, when European powers found themselves too weak to maintain imperial rule, some African countries began making significant headway toward independence. While Ethiopia was the only African country never to be fully colonized, Egypt, Libya, Tunisia, Sudan, Morocco, Ghana, and Guinea all threw off the yoke of their oppressors and became independent in the 1950s. In the 1960s, almost the entire continent followed suit. Unfortunately, all those countries kept the borders established by European powers. This led to a certain amount of instability for many ethnic groups who ended up on multiple sides of the borders. The ethnic conflicts created and perpetrated by colonialists have continued into this period, leading to military rule in many of these countries.

> During the early period of Modern Africa from the early 1960s to the late 1980s, Africa was characterized by more than seventy coups and thirteen presidential assassinations. Border and territorial disputes were also common, with the European-imposed borders of many nations being widely contested through armed conflicts.[162]

In the late 1970s the International Monetary Fund and the World Bank forced governments to enact policies that favored rich elites and starved the poor. Their stated policies supposedly enhanced *development*, but as we've seen all over the world, what actually happened was that these struggling countries continued to be dependent on Western economies. That is why this deplorable dynamic is called *neocolonialism*.

For decades, Ethiopia kept foreign vultures from gaining

1989), p. 163.

162   Fima Lifshitz, *An African Journey Through Its Art* (AuthorHouse, 2009), p. 13.

too much power within their economy by aligning with opposing powers. After World War II, the Cold War between the US and Russia impacted Africa as the superpowers perpetuated internal conflicts and supported inhumane military dictatorships. These tendencies eventually moved to the Ethiopian political landscape, culminating in a "revolution" and Haile Selassie I's ouster. What the people got, however, did not embody democracy. In Campbell's words, "The vast masses were reduced to the limited role of a frightened audience in their own revolution."[163] And in the process, they empowered Mengistu Haile Mariam, who later became known as "the butcher of Addis Ababa."

Even in the 1960s, His Imperial Majesty had been a driver of progressive change. He can be credited with transforming the country from feudalism into the modern age—abolishing slavery and introducing a constitution. Focused on education, he sent many students to the West. Unfortunately, they came back to overthrow him. Biographer Ryszard Kapuściński writes:

The monarch, in spite of his advanced age, maintained a perspicacity amazing to those around him, and he understood better than his closest followers that a new era was coming and it was time to pull together, to bring things up to date, to speed up, to catch up. To catch up, and even to overtake. Yes, he insists, even overtake. He confesses (today one can talk about it) that a part of the Palace was reluctant to embrace these ambitions, muttering privately that instead of giving in to the temptation of certain novelties and reforms, it would be better to curb the Western

---

163   Horace Campbell, *Rasta and Resistance: From Marcus Garvey to Walter Rodney* (Africa World Press, 1987), p. 227.

*inclinations of youth and root out the unreasonable idea
that the country should look different, that it should be
changed.*

*The Emperor, however, listened to neither the aristocratic grumbling nor the university whispers, believing
as he did that all extremes are harmful and unnatural.*[164]

People around Haile Selassie I at the time of his undoing
offer a different story than what Kapuscinski tries to convey—
that Selassie I was some kind of despot. On the contrary, he
chose not to call the troops against his own people when they
tried to overthrow him. In the end, the so-called revolutionaries wreaked havoc on the people they supposedly wanted
to liberate.

The strategic conversion to the Dergue—the Coordinating Committee of the Armed Forces, Police, and Territorial
Army that ruled Ethiopia from 1974 to 1987—began when
their agents started to fill Haile Selassie I's own ranks:

*Their cunning consisted in this: they carried out all their
destruction of the system with the Emperor's name on
their lips, as if executing his will and humbly realizing
his thoughts. Now—claiming to do so in the name of the
Emperor—they created a commission to investigate corruption among dignitaries, checking their accounts, landholdings, and all other riches.*[165]

Haile Selassie's arrest was somewhat anticlimactic, although the significance of the act didn't seem lost on the

164 Ryszard Kapuściński, *The Emperor: Downfall of an Autocrat* (Vintage Books 1989), pgs. 84–85.

165 *Ibid*, p. 132.

official who read the new government's statement to him. As a line of armed soldiers faced the emperor, the man reading the order was shaking, while Selassie I was poised and regal. The Dergue charged him with abuse of power, a lack of competence, and the embezzlement of state funds. Through the media, these charges were spread across the globe, and Selassie I's reputation was tarnished.

After an awkward silence, Selassie I's response to the charges was profound. In the tone of a father speaking to his children, he informed the soldiers that the role of the King of Kings of Ethiopia "is not just a title," it is about "organizing work during peace and defense when under attack," something he had done throughout his life. He reiterated that an individual's desires should never come before the needs of the nation; if it was determined that their actions were for the greater good of Ethiopia, he would comply.[166]

What followed was one of the most horrendous eras in Ethiopia's long history, and the country has still not recovered. Four years after Selassie I was deposed, the "Red Terror" unfolded, leading to "tens of thousands of young people [being] killed, and the government addicted to the use of terror as a weapon of war," according to a report by Africa Watch.[167] The movie *Man of the Millennium: Emperor Haile Selassie I* demonstrates the carnage after the Dergue took power in 1975. "Around 1,500,000 Ethiopians were victims of Dergue genocide," says the filmmaker, "the seventh-worst genocide in world history." Even though Haile Selassie I had been vilified for the famine in the seventies, the "great fam-

---

166 As shown in the movie *Man of the Millennium: Emperor Haile Selassie I* (a Tikher Teferra film, 2008).

167 Africa Watch Report, "Evil Days: 30 Years of War and Famine in Ethiopia" (September 1991), p. 11.

ine" came in the eighties under the Dergue's watch, and was largely attributed to counterinsurgency efforts.

News of Haile Selassie's death prompted Bob Marley to pen the song "Jah Live," singing, "The truth is an offense but not a sin. Is he who laughs last, children, is he who win." The movement of Rastafari focuses on more than just Haile Selassie I's holiness, serving its energies toward individual empowerment and defending inalienable rights.

CHAPTER 7

MUMIA

Oh what a snag, burnt brass hands in the cuffs again,
It's traditional calling the victim a criminal,
Try telling the jury, it's peerless as usual.

This is called a colony, this is called a colony,
Committing those who disagree to a penal colony.

Mumia Abu-Jamal
Was sitting on death row in Pennsylvania,
They'd take his life for the truths he's told,
A writer was sitting on death row for the words he
    wrote.

This is no anomaly, this is no anomaly,
American democracy depends upon a colony.

Mumia Abu-Jamal
Gave sound to those whose voice has been silenced.
In the home of the Liberty Bell
Mumia was felled by a policeman's bullet.

MORE PEOPLE THAN EVER BEHIND BARS

According to Howard Zinn, "The prison had arisen in the United States as an attempt at Quaker reform, to replace mutilation, hanging, exile—the traditional punishments during colonial times."[168] Isolation from society was intended to force inmates to reflect upon their actions and rehabilitate them through self-determination. Instead, this Quaker-inspired isolation bred insanity. Zinn writes that "by the mid-nineteenth century, the prison was based on hard labor, along with various punishments: sweat boxes, iron yokes, solitary. The approach was summed up by the warden at the Ossining, New York Penitentiary: 'In order to reform a criminal you must first break his spirit.' That approach persisted."[169]

The United States incarcerates more people than any other country in the world, and many US prison populations exceed the number of inmates a facility is designed to hold. In 2014, the Sentencing Project analyzed global inmate populations: Rwanda was a distant second to America, Russia was a close third, and Brazil was fourth. In 2014 the US had almost six times the inmate population rate of China.[170]

According to a report by the US Department of Justice, in 2013 almost seven million people were incarcerated, on probation, or on parole. That's nearly 3 percent of the US adult population! And that staggering number represented a decrease from 2007. Unsurprisingly, African Americans were disproportionately represented. Michael Suede states, "If we adopt a more inclusive definition of the criminal class, including all convicted of a felony regardless of imprisonment, these numbers increase to 19.8 million persons, representing 8.6 percent of the adult population and approximately one-third of the African American male population."[171]

---

168 Howard Zinn, *A People's History of the United States* (The New Press, 2003), p. 379.

169 *Ibid*, p. 379.

170 "Fact Sheet: Trends in US Corrections," The Sentencing Project, December 15, 2015, p. 1.

171 Michael Suede, "What Percentage of the US Adult Population Has a Felony Conviction?" *Libertarian News*, June 5, 2014.

Just as worrisome as the huge number of people getting locked up are the eroding rights of ex-convicts. "Once you're labeled a felon," Michelle Alexander writes, "the old forms of discrimination—employment discrimination, housing discrimination, denial of the right to vote, denial of educational opportunity, denial of food stamps and other public benefits, and exclusion from jury service—are suddenly legal." Once someone is labeled a "criminal," they "have scarcely more rights, and arguably less respect, than a black man living in Alabama at the height of Jim Crow. We have not ended racial caste in America, we have merely redesigned it."[172]

To truly illuminate the problems within the national prison system, we must examine inmates' day-to-day lives beyond the obvious cruelty. Prisons often outsource inmates across long distances, making it hard for them to have contact with their relatives and creating a deeper sense of isolation and exile. For example, the state of Hawaii's third-largest prison is in Texas; prisons I visited in North Carolina held inmates from the Virgin Islands.

Jeff Goodman, a software engineer who spent time in prison as a first-time nonviolent offender, offers perspective in his 1998 essay "What a Prison Sentence Really Means." First, he talks about the length of his sentence, imagining what it would be like to hear the judge specifying the actual scope of his punishment. The description compares aspects of being sentenced to an actual version of hell. Getting more specific, Goodman imagines the judge might say, "You'll be stripped of your work skills, your self-worth and your humanity while at the same time face the daily threat of assault, rape, false accusations and unjustified punishment."

---

172 Michelle Alexander, *The New Jim Crow: Mass Incarceration in the Age of Colorblindness* (The New Press, 2010), p. 2.

Although your sentence may be only for a short period of time, you'll be forever stigmatized, and if you manage to re-enter society successfully, "some will say prison was just what you needed . . ." There will be no education programs inside prison designed to reduce recidivism and proven to do so. In fact, "you will live in an environment where recidivism is tacitly encouraged, a fact not lost on those who want to run prisons for profit." Here's more of what the judge might say:

> You are sentenced to consume 150,000 in taxpayer dollars for your prison stay. While lawmakers cite the ever-growing cost of incarceration as a public necessity, you will learn that 10 percent of that amount goes toward your daily needs, while the other 90 percent pays for a bloated prison bureaucracy immune from any cost-benefit analysis. These tax dollars will be siphoned from school programs, child care and job training, all of which do make our communities healthy and safe and save millions in the process . . .[173]

In his essay "The Prison-Industrial Complex," Eric Schlosser reports about illiteracy among prison inmates, as well as the hundreds of thousands who suffer from serious mental illness.

> A generation ago such people were handled primarily by the mental-health, not the criminal-justice system. Sixty to 80 percent of the American inmate population has a history of substance abuse. Meanwhile, the number of drug treatment slots in American prisons has declined by

---

173 Jeff Goodman, "What a Prison Sentence Really Means," *Minneapolis Star Tribune*, December 30, 1998.

more than half since 1993. Drug treatment is now avail-
able to just one in ten of the inmates who need it. Among
those arrested for violent crimes, the proportion who are
African-American men has changed little over the past
twenty years.[174]

Over the course of those two decades, the proportion of African American men who were arrested for drug crimes tripled. "Although the prevalence of illegal drug use among white men is approximately the same as that among black men, black men are five times as like likely to be arrested for a drug offense," Schlosser writes. "The number of women sentenced to a year or more of prison has grown twelvefold since 1970. Of the 80,000 women now imprisoned, about 70 percent are nonviolent offenders and about 75 percent have children."[175]

The origins of this bloated version of the prison-industrial complex can be dated back to the early seventies. At the beginning of the decade, Congress was eliminating federal mandatory minimum sentences for drug offenders and actually closing penitentiaries. But in 1973, Nelson Rockefeller, the governor of New York who had given the order to crush the Attica uprising, "gave a State of the State address demanding that every illegal drug dealer be punished with a mandatory prison sentence of life without parole."[176]

"By proposing the harshest drug laws in the United States," Schlosser continues, Rockefeller "took the lead on an issue that would soon dominate the nation's political agenda." In his State of the State address, Rockefeller ar-

---

174 Eric Schlosser, "The Prison-Industrial Complex," the *Atlantic*, December 1998.

175 *Ibid.*

176 *Ibid.*

gued that "all drug dealers should be imprisoned for life" and "plea-bargaining should be forbidden in such cases and that even juvenile offenders should receive life sentences." This logic, of course, lacks coherence. Someone like Oliver North (the Marine Corps lieutenant colonel who was convicted in the Iran-Contra affair in 1989), who arguably helped decimate many innocent people, didn't risk such sentencing, but petty street "criminals" paid a heavy price. "The penalty for possessing four ounces of an illegal drug, or for selling two ounces, was a mandatory prison term of fifteen years to life."[177]

What comes into question here is not just the laws, but the climate of their enforcement. If laws were enforced equally, drastic measures might have a chance of transforming society, especially if prisons provided educational and vocational opportunities. Yet the massive buildup of security forces at home and abroad is significant, mainly due to the large multinational corporations that seek to squeeze huge profits from "law and order." The media joins the effort by successfully demonizing the individuals in question. In turn, those marginalized "criminals" or "terrorists" are often subjected to inhumane conditions, as if they were enemy combatants in their own country. Unfortunately, even nonviolent offenders suffer from this predicament. Some legal parameters do seem somewhat sensible, especially for violent criminals, government and law enforcement officials who use their office to break laws and officers of large corporations whose crimes affect large numbers of people. Historically, though, the powerful are protected, while petty criminals like drug users and shoplifters are given the cruelest penalties, with long-term ramifications.

---

177 *Ibid.*

As Rockefeller and the media cast these intense penalties for drug crimes as positive and progressive, other states followed suit. No politician wanted to appear soft on crime. As a result, Rockefeller went on to become vice president of the United States under Gerald Ford, Nixon's successor. Simultaneously, as Michelle Alexander explains, the funding to investigate and prosecute white-collar crime was defunded during the inception of the War on Drugs. Authorities and legislators whittled away at the funding for drug treatment, prevention, and education. Also, the "hypersegregation of the black poor in ghetto communities" made targeting such communities easy. "Confined to ghetto areas and lacking political power, the black poor are convenient targets. Douglas Massey and Nancy Denton's book *American Apartheid* documents how racially segregated ghettos were deliberately created by federal policy, not impersonal market forces or private housing choices."[178]

In 2016, even though the US Justice Department issued a memo to end the use of private prisons, the industry had become one of America's fastest-growing economic sectors, generating over $30 billion a year. Although the announcement was met with a certain amount of fanfare, "human rights campaigners and scholars of prisons and criminality [greeted] the announcement with caution . . . While private prisons have been rightfully rebuked for their human rights abuses, they ultimately are not the key driver behind mass incarceration," according to *Washington Post* reporters Zapotosky and Harlan. "The directive is 'limited to the thirteen privately run facilities, housing a little more than 22,000 in-

178 Michelle Alexander, *The New Jim Crow: Mass Incarceration in the Age of Colorblindness* (The New Press, 2010), p. 124.

mates, in the federal Bureau of Prisons system.'"[179] The rising prison-industrial complex was turning people into profit at the expense of their souls and well-being. How disheartening is it that some American children have a greater chance of going to jail than of going to college?

Meanwhile, state and federal inmates generate more profits for private corporations, so lobbyists are chomping at the bit to get more. Trade publications indicate the scope of the prison economy: thousands of vendors offer an amazing array of products, from body scanners to assorted torture devices. Large phone companies make quite a bit of money off of the inmates and their families. MCI was caught adding illegal surcharges to inmate telephone calls; the Department of Corrections received a 32 percent share. There are also food service and health care companies that generate ample profits through their prison services.

The issue isn't solely about privatizing prisons, argues Alex Friedmann, "but rather privatizing prisoners. Inmates, traditionally the responsibility of state and federal governments, increasingly are being contracted out to the lowest bidder. Convicts have become commodities. Certainly offenders should be punished for committing crimes, but should private companies and their stockholders profit from such punishment?"[180] Schlosser brought to light the fact that in 1998, California held "more inmates than France, Great Britain, Germany, Japan, Singapore, and the Netherlands combined."[181]

179 Sarah Lazare, "What You Need to Know About the DOJ's Claim it Is Ending Private Prisons," *Alternet*, August 18, 2016.

180 Alex Friedmann, "Prison Privatization: The Bottom Line," *CorpWatch*, August 21, 1999.

181 Eric Schlosser, "The Prison-Industrial Complex," the *Atlantic*, December 1998.

WHO IS MUMIA ABU-JAMAL?

According to Mumia, "I'm a member and longtime supporter of the MOVE organization and ex-president of the Black Journalist's Association in Philadelphia. I'm still continuing revolutionary journalism. I'm fighting for my life, and fighting to create revolution in America." Mumia was famously sentenced to death by the Philadelphia court of common pleas in July of 1983 after an incident on December 9, 1981, that left a policeman dead and Mumia shot in the stomach.

Mumia started reporting when he was sixteen. As minister of communication for the Philadelphia chapter of the Black Panther Party, he published their newspaper. Although he had no criminal record, his activities generated a 600-page FBI file. In the 1970s he documented many cases of police brutality, especially the Philadelphia Police Department's attacks on MOVE. He was becoming known as the voice of the voiceless and he was detailing what others were scared to report.

As a journalist he posed a threat to the power structure by seeking and telling the truth. And after successfully exposing their corruption, law enforcement officials were apparently determined to put Mumia away. What's striking about his case is the lack of "due process" that an American citizen is supposed to have. Amnesty International reported that the proceedings used to convict and sentence him "were in violation of minimum international standards that govern fair trial procedures," and "that the interests of justice would best be served" by granting him a new trial.[182]

In February 1982, two months after the shooting, a hospital security guard made the assertion that Mumia had issued a "hospital confession." The security guard's stepbrother later

---

182 "USA: A Life in Balance—The Case of Mumia Abu-Jamal," *Amnesty International,* February 2000.

said she'd confided in him that she had lied in court about it. After she made the claim, another hospital guard and two police officers at the scene (including the slain officer's partner) "suddenly 'remembered' they had also heard the alleged 'confession' . . . However, the officer guarding Mumia at the hospital wrote on the day of the shooting that Mumia 'made no comment.'"[183] This string of obvious falsehoods reflected a pattern followed in many of the cases against political and social activists in the sixties and seventies. At Mumia's trial, Judge Albert F. Sabo refused to recess court to bring in the officer guarding Mumia at the hospital on the day of the shooting. Even the medical examiner's report, which identified the fatal bullet as a different caliber than Mumia's, was not made available at the trial. Judge Sabo refused Mumia's constitutional right to defend himself, and the prosecution's star witness may have been persuaded by the combination of her previous thirty-eight convictions and the several cases still open against her. Other prosecution witnesses testified that she wasn't even at the scene of the crime. "The police didn't need evidence," Terry Bisson writes. "They didn't need to secure the crime scene, or follow their own procedures. They had the man they wanted. The rest was a mere formality."[184]

The very nature of Mumia's incarceration points to a serious flaw within the US criminal justice system: those who meted out the penalties advanced their careers, while those falsely incarcerated were left to languish in taxpayer-funded gulags. An unattributed brochure in support of Mumia says it best: "We must save Mumia not only because he tells the

183 Betsey Piette, "Supreme Court Denies Mumia Right to Present New Witnesses," *Workers World*, October 18, 2008.

184 Terry Bisson, *On a Move: The Story of Mumia Abu-Jamal* (Litmus Books, 2000), p. 182.

truth about the system. We must also save him to spare thousands of others who are in danger of being next."

After more than three decades of incarceration, Mumia continues his work. He had a radio show on NPR called *Live from Death Row*, but in 1994 Senator Bob Dole threatened to cut NPR's funding if they did not cancel it. Mumia has since spoken remotely at multiple college commencement ceremonies; he gave the commencement address at Evergreen College in 1999, Antioch in 2000, and at Goddard, where Mumia went to school, in 2014.

POLITICAL PRISONERS IN THE USA

Angela Davis, a university professor who has worked on behalf of prison abolition, wrote the profoundly important book *Are Prisons Obsolete?* She examines the growth of US prisons, institutions that were initially intended to dole out humane, measured justice. Yet we have noticeably strayed from that goal. Innocent people are sent to prison for self-medicating, practicing self-defense and defending others, and simply speaking out against the powers that be.

In an article written from prison, Davis succinctly describes this dilemma: "There is a distinct and qualitative difference between one breaking a law for one's own individual self-interest and violating it in the interests of a class of people whose oppression is expressed either directly or indirectly through that particular law." Then she adds, "The former might be called a criminal (though in many cases he is a victim), but the latter, as a reformist or revolutionary, is interested in universal social change. Captured, he or she is a political prisoner."[185]

Since the social upheavals of the sixties, the number of

---

185   Angela Y. Davis, "Political Prisoners, Prisons, and Black Liberation," *History Is a Weapon* website, May 1971.

political prisoners in the US has grown dramatically. In 1978, when Andrew Young was the US ambassador to the UN, he made a controversial public statement about political prisoners: "We still have hundreds of people that I would categorize as political prisoners in our prisons."[186] That large number referred to activists serving short stints, and the reaction was swift. Congressman Larry McDonald immediately tried to have Young removed from office.

By far the most aggressive and resourceful weapon against these activists was the FBI's COINTELPRO program, which ruthlessly hunted down and even killed dissidents. Other activists were humiliated; they were stripped naked in front of the press and beaten mercilessly. Regarding these atrocities, Dhoruba Bin Wahad remarks, "COINTELPRO, as implemented by the FBI, was aimed at countering the rise in political power of a domestic national minority—specifically, primarily, black people . . ." It "transcended mere investigation. It was in effect a domestic war program . . . waged by a government against a people, against its own citizens."[187] J. Soffiyah Elijah, a clinical instructor at the Criminal Justice Institute of Harvard Law School who represented Marilyn Buck and Sundiata Acoli in court, succinctly summarizes COINTELPRO's impacts:

> Before COINTELPRO was laid to rest, it was responsible for maiming, murdering, false prosecutions and frame-ups, destruction, and mayhem throughout the country. It had infiltrated every organization and associa-

186   Andrew J. DeRoche, *Andrew Young: Civil Rights Ambassador* (Rowman and Littlefield, 2003), p. 102.

187   Joy James, *Warfare in the American Homeland: Policing and Prison in a Penal Democracy* (Duke University Press, 2007), p. 80.

tion that aspired to bring about social change in America whether through peaceful or violent means. Hundreds of members of the Puerto Rican independence movement, the Black Panther Party, the Young Lords, the Weather Underground, Students for a Democratic Society, the Republic of New Africa, the Student Nonviolent Coordinating Committee, members of the American Indian Movement, the Chicano movement, the Black Liberation Army, environmentalists, the Revolutionary Action Movement, peace activists, and everyone in between were targeted by COINTELPRO for "neutralization."[188]

Elijah addresses an issue that repeatedly undermines our democracy—the targeting of lawyers who represent controversial clients. She says that being involved in such cases "usually finds the lawyer on the receiving end of constant harassment from prison and jail officials, federal marshals, court personnel and prosecutors[189] . . . How else can we explain the recent and unprecedented arrest and indictment of New York lawyer Lynn Stewart, a zealous advocate well respected amongst members of the bar and the bench?"[190]

Prosecutors and courts traditionally comply with the FBI and their devious tactics. "Prosecutors routinely withheld exculpatory evidence as was evidenced in the cases of Geronimo Ji-Jaga Pratt, Dhoruba Bin Wahad, and Mumia Abu-Jamal. Although Pratt and Bin Wahad were eventually exonerated after serving twenty-seven and nineteen years respectively for crimes they did not commit, requests by Peltier

---

188 J. Soffiyah Elijah, "The Reality of Political Prisoners in the United States: What September 11 Taught Us About Defending Them," *Harvard BlackLetter Law Journal*, Vol. 18, 2002, pgs. 130–131.

189 *Ibid*, p. 133.

190 *Ibid*, p. 134.

and Abu-Jamal for new trials have been frustrated at every turn by law enforcement and the prosecution."[191]

Some of the political activists sent to prison by the FBI's COINTELPRO program were isolated and monitored in new facilities designed especially for sensory deprivation and behavior-modification techniques, otherwise known as torture. Sundiata Acoli was interviewed in 1996 while serving time in FCC Allenwood, and he spoke about what happened in 1975 in the New Jersey prison system. He described how unannounced, the guards rounded up 250 inmates and relocated them overnight. They had to leave their property behind. In the pre–Civil War facility, their cells were so small that "you could outstretch your arms and touch both walls." Acoli reflected how he considered it a "smokescreen to round up about fifty or sixty either Political Prisoners or prisoners that were involved in African study classes . . ." They were no longer allowed contact visits, library access, or any meaningful recreation. They had to spend twenty-three hours and fifty minutes a day in those cells.[192]

Prisons are increasingly being used as tools of counterinsurgency by a US government facing serious economic, social, political, and military crises. In 2003, Bernardine Dohrn from the Weather Underground was quoted in the *Asheville Global Report* newspaper about the scope of this issue: "The mass incarceration of people of color took place through a very deliberate cultivation of fear, the legend of a crime wave, and the invention of the super-predator myth during a decade when crime rates plummeted."[193]

---

191 *Ibid*, p. 131.

192 Bonnie Kerness and Sundiata Acoli, "Uses and Effects of Control Unit Prisons," 1996, pgs. 1–2.

193 Bernardine Dohrn, "Homeland Imperialism: Fear and Resistance," *Monthly Review*, Volume 55, Issue 3, July/August 2003.

By incarcerating an unprecedented number of people in our penal system, the US government has selected the most expensive social and legal reform option available to them, but also, and more problematically, the prison-industrial complex supports significant human suffering and misspends public funds. According to a 2012 report by the Vera Institute of Justice, "The total per-inmate cost averaged $31,286 [annually] and ranged from $14,603 in Kentucky to $60,076 in New York."[194] Now imagine if that money was instead the salary inmates could earn for being productive members of society. In 2012, the total annual price taxpayers paid for incarceration was $63.4 billion.[195]

Echoing Michelle Alexander in *The New Jim Crow*, Bernardine Dohrn elucidates that "the legacy of slavery, the modern-day version of slavery, is reflected one way in prisons but it is also visible in the transformation of schools. Schools in America have become barricaded places of fear."[196] When I accompanied one of my daughters to her first day of middle school, I recognized the school's floor plan because it was identical to a prison I had visited with the Rastafari Univer-Soul Fellowship. Indeed, according to Dohrn,

> *People who don't have their own youngsters in school today may not realize what's happened to the environment where our young people spend seven hours of their day . . . The fear of violence and the notion that it is likely to come from anywhere, including from our young people, has been the precursor and the trial run for what's now*

---

194 Christian Henrichson and Ruth Delany, "The Price of Prisons: What Incarceration Costs Taxpayers," Vera Institute of Justice, February 2012.

195 Martha Teichner, "The Cost of a Nation of Incarceration," CBS News, April 23, 2013.

196 Bernardine Dohrn, "Homeland Imperialism: Fear and Resistance," *Monthly Review*, Volume 55, Issue 3, July/August 2003.

happened in all of our public spaces and airports . . . Now
we have war abroad and war at home.[197]

RASTAFARI UNIVERSOUL FELLOWSHIP PRISON MINISTRY

Ganja, the sacramental herb of Rastafari, is of course still illegal in most US states and the War on Drugs continues unabated. Michelle Alexander helps debunk myths regarding the horrendous military campaign against everyday people. "The first is that the war is aimed at ridding the nation of drug 'kingpins' or big-time dealers. Nothing could be further from the truth," she says. "The vast majority of those arrested are *not* charged with serious offenses." She explains that 80 percent of the drug arrests in 2005 were for possession and that only 20 percent were for selling the substances. "Moreover," she writes, "most people in state prison for drug offenses have *no* history of violence or significant selling activity."

The second myth she destroys is that "the drug war is principally concerned with dangerous drugs. Quite to the contrary, arrests for marijuana possession—a drug less harmful that tobacco or alcohol—accounted for nearly 80 percent of the growth in drug arrests in the 1990s."[198] Of course, not all inmates we served with the Rastafari UniverSoul Fellowship were locked up on possession charges; others were interested in finding out more about Rastafari regardless of their sentencing. But Rastas are easy for law enforcement to target and convict.

In 2011, I was pulled over thirteen times in one month when an ICE (Immigration and Customs Enforcement)

---

197 *Ibid.*

198 Michelle Alexander, *The New Jim Crow: Mass Incarceration in the Age of Colorblindness* (The New Press, 2010), p. 60.

checkpoint was set up near the house I was living in, outside Asheville. It was presumably established to catch undocumented workers; there was a factory nearby that had recently been raided by ICE.[199] But despite my other neighbors' non-issues with the ICE agents at the checkpoint, I was repeatedly asked for my license and registration. One time I asked the officer: "Don't you remember me from yesterday?" "Just show me your license," he replied. Two times he asked me to step out of the vehicle so he could search the car. I complied the first time, but the second time I respectfully declined. I didn't have to wonder what would have happened if I had misplaced my license or my registration was past due, or if I happened to have some herb on me.

I have had the unique opportunity to meet with H.I.H. Prince Ermias Sahle Selassie, Haile Selassie I's grandson, at the Smithsonian Institute in DC. Jake Homiak, the Smithsonian's director of the National Anthropological Archives, was also present. There were multiple agendas going on that day, but H.I.H. noticeably perked up when we informed him about our work within the prison system. Ras Miles Jacob Marley, an ordained minister, started the Rastafari Univer-Soul Fellowship in Florida after inmates requested him to do so. He was a reggae DJ at the time and the prisoners tuning in to his show informed him of the violence occurring between different factions of Rastafari brethren. Once he met them personally, they asked that he represent a "universal perspective" to bring unity to the Rastas in prison from different mansions of the faith.

---

199 Staff, "What 'Immigration Enforcement' Looks Like in North Carolina: Pulled Over 13 Times in One Month at an Immigration Checkpoint," *Fight Back News*, February 15, 2013.

Rastafari is a recognized "religion" within the US prison system, so Rastas have the same rights of worship as any other recognized religion. Members of RUF (including myself) were able to visit prisons ranging from minimum to maximum security, in order to conduct "religious services" for the brethren. That means we could bring in drums and spend the day with them, chanting, reasoning, and playing music. At North Carolina's Marion Correctional Center, we brought two reggae artists from the Virgin Islands—Niyorah and Bamboo Station. We even once brought two Rastafari elders—Binghi Irie Lion from the Nyahbinghi mansion and Priest Haile Israel from the band Ras Michael and the Sons of Negus. Seeing the prisoners reason with elders from Jamaica was a moving experience; it even brought tears to Binghi Irie's eyes.

One time at a maximum-security facility in South Carolina, we brought our drum delegation clad in red, gold, and green and stepped into a prison yard of around three hundred inmates. We got salutes and smiles from many as we ventured down the walkway leading to the chapel. This was a facility whose Christian priest was called Chaplain One Love. He was a Jámaican who had met Haile Selassie I as a child. The prisoners and chaplains have frequently told us that our spiritual services are the only services that draw people from multiple faiths. At our events we have adherents of Judaism, Islam, Moorish Science Temple, multiple denominations of Christianity, Native Americans, atheists, and others attending. Many are inspired by Haile Selassie I's inclusivity. Working with inmates is incredibly fulfilling because the need is so great. In no other part of my life have I experienced such appreciation.

The lack of connection between prisoners and the outside world is a huge part of why recidivism remains high. The desperation one can feel inside these complexes—even for those working there—is significant. The prisons administrations' own literature says the best way to help prisoners become reacclimated to society is for the community to visit them as much as possible before their release. As we navigated the protocols, we came in contact with many who were teaching meditation, art, music, and other expressive outlets.

A great success RUF experienced during my time there was helping to shepherd the release of Stephen Smith. He, of course, deserves all the credit—we were merely instruments of his initiative. He was a member of the Rasta group in the Marion prison. He had served almost seventeen years; his final stint was in a minimum-security facility near where I lived. After he was released, he started his own landscaping business, served on the board of my co-op, and advocated for reentry rights in North Carolina. He is very passionate about helping inmates return to society and stay out of their cells for good.

Prisons could truly become incubators for creative innovation. Millions of talented people languish behind bars; with the right direction, many inmates could become future leaders and innovators. Vocational and recreational endeavors complement each other. Prisons should become farms, job training facilities, music schools, technical colleges, craft schools, etc. The possibilities are endless. And instead of making pennies on the dollar, inmates should be able to earn real wages, so that they may learn the true value of an honest day's work. Some inmates are already making this happen.

CO-OPS IN PRISONS

I never imagined that working in a cooperative, I would find the ideal model to rehabilitate myself.[200]
—Roberto Rodriguez

Dr. Jessica Gordon Nembhard helped educate me about co-ops in prisons. I had heard about the phenomenon but never experienced it, and finding information online was difficult. In Cuba, longtime cooperative educator Anne Hoyt and I often ate breakfast together. At our breakfast table, I learned about her travels around the world. She had discovered that people in other countries were surprised to learn that there were so many co-ops in the US. But according to the National Co+op Grocers, "There are more than 29,000 co-ops in the United States with Americans holding 350 million co-op memberships." Also, "The majority of our country's 2 million farmers are members of the nearly 3,000 farmer-owned cooperatives. They provide over 250,000 jobs and annual wages of over $8 billion."[201]

Unfortunately, there are still no co-ops in US prisons that I know of. But one of our country's "possessions" in the Caribbean—Puerto Rico—has implemented co-ops within their prison system. Lymarie Nieves, a marketing director at a credit union on the island, is so inspired by her work with prison co-ops that she has made it her life's mission to serve as a spokesperson for what she calls "transformational cooperativism."

---

200   Meegan Moriarty, "From Bars to Freedom: Prisoner Co-ops Boost Employment, Self-Esteem and Support Re-Entry into Society," *Rural Cooperatives*, January/February 2016, p. 18.

201   "Co-op FAQs and Facts," *Co-op, Stronger Together,* http://strongertogether.coop/food-coops/co-op-faqs-and-facts.

She first made contact with Roberto Rodriguez and the Cooperativa ARIGOS because she wanted to write an article about the group. Then she began teaching them cooperative principles, philosophy, and history. Thus, what is likely the world's first prisoner worker co-op started as a self-motivated mental health program rather than an income stream. Hector Quiñones, Efrain Oriz, and Santos Villaran started an arts and crafts collective in 1993 "to keep their minds together." Rodriguez became the secretary of the co-op. As he tells it, the road to incorporation was not an easy one, but surprisingly, the governor was willing to allow their continuance and the law was amended, so four prisoner co-ops sprang up in Puerto Rico. Rodriguez is now out of prison and has traveled with Nieves to Worcester and Amherst, Massachusetts, as well as to Berkeley and Oakland, California, to spread the gospel that will improve the nation's prisons.

The entire Puerto Rican cooperative movement supported them, even holding an exhibition for the prisoners. Through the co-ops the prisoners exhibit their work at co-op events, and sell their wares. The board and cooperative members attend cooperative events with two guards. Nieves lobbied the correctional system to gain respect for the co-op and allow them to work by themselves. She helped to educate the co-op members inside the prison, organized government meetings so that the members could present their projects, served as the group's spokesperson in the co-op movement, and helped with marketing and seeking support from other cooperatives.[202]

---

202 Ajowa Nzinga Ifateyo, "The World's First Prisoner Worker Co-op: Transforming Prisoner's Lives Through Cooperation in Puerto Rico," *Grassroots Economic Organizing*, September 16, 2015.

Gordon Nembhard argues that beyond their market value, co-ops "provide leadership development, financial education and literacy, high-level social skills and collective decision-making."[203] These are highly needed components for inmates to successfully reenter society. Most importantly, in a better system prisoners could shorten their terms by working in co-ops, which might produce a tangible drop in recidivism. In Italy, one of the participants pointed out that "80 percent return to prison, in general, but for those employed by a social co-operative the recidivism rate drops to less than 10 percent"[204] Anne Hoyt's research has found that prisoner cooperatives are very "cost-effective," and with the "deep commitment on the part of the Italians to the rehabilitation of prisoners," roughly "10 percent of prisoners in Italy participate in prisoner cooperatives."[205]

Before I coincidentally met up with her in Cuba, Gordon Nembhard had visited my hometown for a speaking engagement, and I spoke with her briefly afterward. When I told her about the various statements Haile Selassie I had made about the value of co-ops, she was already aware; she was, in fact, preparing to visit Ethiopia to learn about their prison co-ops. Here's a related passage that I later found in the USDA's *Rural Cooperatives* magazine:

> *Convicts at Ethiopia's Mekelle Prison have formed more than 20 cooperatives through which they perform various*

203 Betsy Dribben, "Social Cooperatives and Prison Systems," *Co-op News*, November 2015.

204 *Ibid.*

205 Meegan Moriarty, "From Bars to Freedom: Prisoner Co-ops Boost Employment, Self-Esteem and Support Re-Entry into Society," *Rural Cooperatives*, January/February 2016, p. 16.

forms of work, including farming, carpentry, plumbing, electric work and handicrafts. An Ethiopian banking institution provides loans to prisoners to start cooperatives, and the loans are guaranteed by the prison. Prisoners use wages for restitution to victims and to invest back into the cooperatives.[206]

Clearly there is a lot of opportunity for America, "the world's incarcerator," to develop co-ops within the prison system.

---

206 *Ibid*, p. 17.

CHAPTER 8

KEN SARO-WIWA

Ken Saro-Wiwa lived in Nigeria,
Ken was no crony, he came from Ogoni.
Ken Saro-Wiwa worked in the media,
Shell Oil played a lethal hand when they destroyed his
    homeland.

That wasn't his company,
That wasn't his government,
Those aren't his people
Running Royal Dutch Shell.

They hire private armies,
They have a foreign policy,
They're making Dutch money
On African oil.

Ken Saro-Wiwa, killed in Nigeria,
Not for Nigerians but for the Netherlands.
Ken Saro-Wiwa, crucified by hysteria,
While they made grand after grand, they destroyed his
    homeland.

How long will they plunder his homeland?
Though they're wrong, they seem to have the upper hand.
Ken's gone because oil's in demand.
With this song, we remember the man.

Ken Saro-Wiwa met his end in Nigeria,
Wouldn't take their male deal, wouldn't have his nation
    kneel,
Ken Saro-Wiwa.

Kenule Beeson Saro-Wiwa was born in Bori on the southern coast of Nigeria. He was a university instructor, grocer, writer of novels, plays, poems, television scripts, and children's books, and a renowned columnist for three different Lagos daily newspapers. Ken's tribal homeland is often called Ogoniland, although he wrote in his book *A Month and a Day: A Detention Diary* that he prefers the term *Ogoni*. He explained, "To the Ogoni, the land and the people are one and are expressed as such in our local languages."[207]

Ogoni is in the Niger Delta, a hotspot for oil barons who control Nigeria's vast oil reserves. Since the mid-1950s, Ogoni has been decimated by industrial pollution resulting from oil extraction. According to William Boyd, who wrote the introduction to Saro-Wiwa's detention diary, "What was once a placid rural community of prosperous farmers and fisherman is now an ecological wasteland reeking of sulphur, its creeks and waterholes poisoned by indiscriminate oil spillage and ghoulishly lit at night by the orange flames of gas flares."[208]

In America, pipelines are often located beside highways and roads, but Ogoni's ran right down the middle of the dirt streets lined with homes. The oil companies installed the pumps without considering public safety, which meant pumps roiled in the center of towns, forcing children to play in the inevitable spillage. Royal Dutch Shell effectively turned Nigeria into an occupied territory.

Ken resisted the oil company. He held them responsible for their ecological calamities, attesting that they were contributing to a "slow genocide" that devastated his people. He openly protested this despoliation and demanded com-

---

207 Ken Saro-Wiwa, *A Month and a Day: A Detention Diary* (Penguin Books, 1995), p. 2.

208 *Ibid*, p. x.

pensation from the Nigerian government and from the international oil companies benefitting from their land. Since the government and private corporations were already accustomed to working together, committing crimes far worse than anything Ken was ever accused of, it was easy for them to team up to bring about his demise.

In May 1994, four Ogoni leaders suspected of collaborating with the military were killed at a rally. Saro-Wiwa was prevented from attending because of a military roadblock. He was arrested anyway, along with fifteen others, and accused of incitement to murder. Imprisoned for more than a year, he was tried before a specially convened tribunal, which included a representative from Royal Dutch Shell. "On Thursday, November 2, [1995], Ken and eight co-defendants were found guilty and sentenced to death. Suddenly the world acknowledged the nature of Nigerian degeneracy," [209] and the power of a corporation over a nation.

At the end of the eighties, while recording an album with my band Soulside outside of Amsterdam, I learned about this devastation in Ogoni. I followed the resistance movement's progress because I had been involved in the anti-Apartheid demonstrations in college in the 1980s. I was completely blown away when I learned of Saro-Wiwa's story, not simply because he was a peace activist essentially executed by a corporation, but because I was made aware of his suffering during real time. George Jackson's writing about global capital and its fascist nature were ringing in my head. I was astounded by the stark reality of these insidious corporate endeavors.

---

209 *Ibid*, p. xiii.

DID FASCISM WIN WORLD WAR II?

George Jackson wrote of monopoly capital in America at the end of the Civil War. "Prior to its emergence," he explained, "bourgeois democratic rule could be said to have been the predominant political force inside Amerikan society. As monopoly capital matured, the role of the old bourgeois democracy faded in the process. As monopoly capital forced out the small dispersed factory setup, the new corporativism assumed political supremacy."[210]

Jackson saw fascism as a core component of capitalism, especially when the economic system is in a state of crisis. What's easy to miss is that even though its expression has nationalist qualities, fascism is ultimately an international movement, as Jackson points out. Most ominously, he wrote, "The ultimate aim of fascism is the complete destruction of all revolutionary consciousness."[211]

Because of struggling economies in the 1930s, developed government "heroes" stepped in to "save" developing countries. "The key element that made the economic policy of fascist arrangements unique was the emphasis on 'reform through government intervention,'" wrote Jackson. He contended that this brand of fascism flourished after World War II: "reforms" meant corporations forcing the government to act, or forcing the government not to act and thereby uphold their international policies. Jackson argued that the US slipped into international fascism by merging "the economic, political, and labor elites."[212]

Reaganomics worsened international conditions due to the neoliberal economic polices shaped by Milton Friedman.

---

210   George L. Jackson, *Blood in My Eye* (Black Classic Press, 1996), p. 136.

211   *Ibid*, p. 137.

212   *Ibid*, p. 164.

The United States Agency for International Development, the International Monetary Fund, and the World Bank intervened in Nigeria, post-Apartheid South Africa, and Eastern Europe after the fall of the Berlin Wall. Naomi Klein gives a detailed account of the vast array of related misdeeds in her book *The Shock Doctrine*:

> The movement that Milton Friedman launched in the 1950s is best understood as an attempt by multinational capital to recapture the highly profitable, lawless frontier that Adam Smith, the intellectual forefather of today's neoliberals, so admired—but with a twist. Rather than journeying through Smith's "savage and barbarous nations" where there was no Western law (no longer a practical option), this movement set out to systematically dismantle existing laws and regulations to re-create that earlier lawlessness. And where Smith's colonists earned their record profits by seizing what he described as "waste lands" for "but a trifle," today's multinationals see government programs, public assets and everything that is not for sale as terrain to be conquered and seized—the post office, national parks, schools, social security, disaster relief and anything else that is publicly administered.[213]

Such Friedmanite interventions made President Franklin Delano Roosevelt's New Deal and the Marshall Plan look generous. Domestically, FDR contended with formidable popular forces demanding economic independence. "In the 1932 presidential elections, one million Americans voted

---

213 Naomi Klein, *The Shock Doctrine: The Rise of Disaster Capitalism* (Picador, 2008), pgs. 304–305.

for Socialist or Communist candidates"[214]; many years later, avowed Socialist Bernie Sanders nearly nabbed the Democratic presidential nomination. But in the 2016 presidential election, more was needed to stem the tide of parasitic neoliberal forces. In Eastern Europe, neoliberals easily forced through much less cooperative initiatives because Russia had been transformed away from a Communist entity; Klein notes that "capitalism was suddenly free to lapse into its most savage form, not just in Russia but around the world."[215]

Soulside's 1989 tour took me to many locations discussed in *The Shock Doctrine*. The Iron Curtain had not yet come down, and drastic changes were about to be made in many Eastern Europe economies. We played in East Berlin and Poland six months before the Berlin Wall came down; we were in Yugoslavia just before it was torn apart by war. Things were heating up fast, so we drove straight through Kosovo and around Albania to reach Greece. Our travels in these countries felt timely and eye-opening, reflecting the tremendous amount of revolutionary activity happening around the globe.

At that time, going behind the Iron Curtain meant walking into completely different lifestyles from Western Europe and America. WWII-era bullet holes dotted the architecture. Goods were traded solely with the East, so there were no bananas in the markets, for example. In Poland, we played in cultural centers that looked like museums. We arrived a couple of weeks before the first free Parliament election, which eventually brought the Solidarity Party to power. On the way to Poland, we played an illegal show in East Berlin at a Protestant church. This was special and rare because punk

---

214   *Ibid*, p. 316.
215   *Ibid*, p. 318.

rock was strictly forbidden at that time in East Germany.

One thing that immediately struck me in Poland was that even before Lech Wałesa and the Solidarity Party gained political power, the punks we talked to were already disillusioned with the movement. Kline states that these societies entered the global economy on neoliberal terms and were plagued by a central dynamic: although people could exercise political power, their governments had already signed away their economies. Without economic power, political power meant very little, as evidenced in South Africa when Nelson Mandela and the African National Congress assumed leadership in 1994.

The folks in the punk scene who brought us to Poland were given credit for teaching the Solidarity Movement about techniques in independent media, specifically via a fanzine called *Antena Krzyku*. In the eighties, it was one of the best-known underground Polish zines covering independent music and counterculture on both sides of the Iron Curtain. It was totally independent, which in late-Communist Poland also meant illegal, and it became somewhat of a nucleus for the Polish DIY community, leading up to the rise of Solidarity and the fall of the Berlin Wall.

NIGERIA AND THE GLOBAL ECONOMY IN THE 1970S

The whole of Nigeria, like many of the countries afflicted by the policies of the World Bank and the IMF, endured a similar dynamic as what was happening in Ogoni, for companies like Shell were making huge profits and trickling just enough income to government tyrants in order to keep them happy. Naturally, none of the profits reached the people. For example, in 1978 Nigeria had borrowed $5 billion from the

IMF, and by 2000 "had reimbursed $16 billion, but still owed $31 billion, according to President Obasanjo."[216] The loan seemed to have been set up to cripple their economy.

> *Indeed, it is the IMF and World Bank that have dictated that Nigeria should focus its spending on debt servicing; rather than on education and health care. They are responsible for forcing Nigeria to liberalize every aspect of the economy. This has seen the Nigerian state clamping down on workers' rights; privatizing every government function including health care and education; relaxing environmental laws; and allowing multinational corporations to repatriate all of their profits out of Nigeria. All of this has been done in order to meet the desires of the multinational oil companies that are operating in Nigeria; at the direct expense of the majority of people.*[217]

The global capitalist economy from WWII up to the early 1970s was known as "regulated capitalism." It had encouraged a period of sustained growth around the world. The expectation was that it would continue, but in the early 1970s global economic growth fell to half of what it had been previously. This prompted the US to internally abolish fixed exchange rates, which in turn changed the roles of the World Bank and the IMF.

Both of these institutions were created to help rebuild Europe after WWII. They were established as part of the Bretton Woods Agreement to administer loans and main-

---

216 Demba Moussa Dembele, "The International Monetary Fund and World Bank in Africa: A 'Disastrous' Record," *Pambazuka News: Voices for Freedom and Justice*, September 23, 2004.

217 Shawn Hattingh, "A Shell of Democracy," Royal Dutch Shell PLC, May 25, 2007.

tain fixed exchange rates for all currencies. After 1972, they focused on the so-called third world, requiring nations to accept structural adjustment programs, which lowered minimum wages, raised food costs, and ultimately failed their economies, causing them to be, among other things, reliant on foreign powers rather than remain self-sufficient. In Africa, corporations easily stepped in after the demise of colonialism.

Newly formed independent governments struggled to adapt to the globalization of their economies. Taking on debt seemed like their only path, and the "experts" assured them that it would be worth the risk. Unfortunately, the way countries' borders were partitioned during colonialism also assured ongoing domestic social strife, as was evident in Nigeria after independence in 1960. The atmosphere set in motion a series of military coups, and dictatorial leadership flourished, morphing into what Ken Saro-Wiwa dubbed "domestic colonialism." Speaking on behalf of the Ogoni in a 1992 presentation to the UN's Working Group on Indigenous Populations, Saro-Wiwa said:

> The nation which the British left behind was supposed to be a federal democracy, but the federating ethnic nations were bound by few agreements and the peoples were so disparate, so culturally different, so varied in size, that force and violence seemed to be the only way of maintaining the nation. In the circumstances, the interests of the few and weak such as the Ogoni were bound to suffer and have suffered.[218]

---

218 Ken Saro-Wiwa, A Month and a Day: A Detention Diary (Penguin Books, 1996), p. 95.

After a devastating civil war in Nigeria at the end of the 1960s, which largely revolved around controlling oil-bearing land, the ensuing "oil boom of the 1970s profoundly transformed Nigerian society from one based on agricultural exports to one based on exports of crude oil . . . Oil money was appropriated by indigenous capitalists who tended to invest abroad rather than locally. Much theft was geared toward conspicuous consumption and land acquisition."[219] This devastated the smaller ethnic groups like the Ogoni, who had lived in the Niger Delta for generations.

After serving in numerous governmental posts, Saro-Wiwa became intensely active in setting up a nonviolent movement to defend his people's rights and the rights of other marginalized ethnic groups. The Movement for the Survival of the Ogoni People was formed, and Saro-Wiwa promptly drafted an Ogoni Bill of Rights, which detailed the movement's demands: a fair share of the oil money made from their land, and a cleanup of the environmental damage the oil companies meted out.

Their plight was shaky at best, because grabbing their land had already been a primary focus during the civil war from 1967 to 1970. The postwar Nigerian Constitution ensured ethnic minorities living on or near mineral resources—oil—would have no real voice in Parliament, where the decision rested for the land's sale. The minorities were dealing with a stronger central government that was completely dependent on oil. As a result, significant demonstrations flared up.

A newly radicalized Fela Kuti was determined to use his music as a weapon to expose Nigeria's corporate and government corruption. Fela had been a jazz musician in London

---

219 Terisa E. Turner with Bryan J. Ferguson, *Arise Ye Mighty People!: Gender, Class and Race in Popular Struggles* (Africa World Press, 1994), pgs. 133–134.

and his unchartered musical innovation led him to Los Angeles, where he was exposed to the Black Panthers and the Black Power movement. Fela soon became the father of Afro Beat, a musical genre so infectious that it gave the singer an international platform to express the people's dissatisfaction with government *and* global corporations. In his song "International Thief Thief," Fela chanted:

> *Many foreign companies dey Africa carry all our money*
> *go . . .*
> *Them get one style wey them dey use. Them go pick one*
> *African man—a man with low mentality . . .*
> *Him go bribe some thousand naira bread to become one*
> *useless chief . . .*

Fela's son Seun Kuti later penned a song called "IMF," dubbing the institution an "International Mother Fucker." It was clear to most Nigerians that their oppression was based not just on the whims of local despots, but also on the greed of corporate interlopers. The culture of capitalism that abounded not only aggravated ethnic relations, it also exacerbated gender relations. In Nigeria, though, women were not having it.

WOMEN'S UPRISINGS IN NIGERIA

In *Arise Ye Mighty People*, Turner and Oshare point to the inherent marginalization of women in the global realization of capitalism. The authors speak of a "class formation," in which gender roles are altered to fit the new economic model, elevating the role of men in the society at the expense of the women. Moving the conversation forward and looking at the results on the ground, Turner and Oshare are quick to determine that "alliances of solidarity between women and men are prerequisites for overcoming the power of capital and for organizing an egalitarian, cooperative society."[220]

The story of women's uprisings in Nigeria is stunning. In the eighties, women led two revolts against the oil industry. The earlier uprising in 1984 was more successful because the women confronted the subsidiary of a US company directly, without the state or the coopted chiefs coming between them. The 1986 Ekpan uprising differed, and so did the results. The decisive victory in 1984 of the smaller-scale Ogharefe women's uprising benefitted from the support of the influential Council of Youth, as well as from men in their community. Yet women didn't hand over leadership to these men, which Turner and Oshare place into a historical context. "Throughout the twentieth century," they write, "Nigerian women have exercised the social power under their control in their own interests, and in the interests of the community."[221]

As the post–civil war state sector grew, women's spheres of economic activity suffered. Following a government decree in 1977, land not privately owned was confiscated by the federal government. The "male deal" meant the state formally recognized certain chiefs who supported the move, as detailed in Fela Kuti's song "International Thief Thief." This pitted the chiefs against their people, which worked in favor of the state and private companies in cahoots with the foreign oil industry. These factors eventually led to the 1984 uprising.

Highlighting the resourcefulness of the oppressed, one

---

220 Terisa E. Turner with Bryan J. Ferguson, *Arise Ye Mighty People!: Gender, Class and Race in Popular Struggles* (Africa World Press, 1994), p. 130.

221 *Ibid*, p. 131.

of the main weapons the women used against their foes was nakedness. In their culture, "disrobing by women in public is considered a serious and permanent curse on those to whom the women expose themselves," which meant that a "foreign man subjected to this curse would lose his credibility (potency) in Nigeria and would be effectively neutralized."[222]

The people of Ogharefe had not been compensated for their land, which was sold to a subsidiary of Pan Ocean, a US multinational corporation. The people also suffered "from skin rashes, stomach ailments and other health problems associated with hundreds of 24-hour-a-day natural gas flares and the discharge of 'oil production water' into the environment."[223] The women demanded payment for the land and a free supply of well water and electricity. Their initial protests were unsuccessful, so they took things to the next level. Early one morning, thousands of women descended on the grounds of the Ogharefe Production Station and effectively prevented the next shift of workers from assuming their posts. When the Pan Ocean managing director showed up on the scene, the women had already taken off their clothes: "The sight of thousands of naked women of all ages was not one that these officials nor the police could withstand. They all fled without hesitation. The women's demands were met almost immediately."[224]

This was a powerful form of direct action. Previous to the next uprising, there had been a very successful tax protest, where a multiclass mobilization made it possible for people to defeat a key element of the IMF's structural adjustment program. The IMF was forced to withdraw its directive to

222   Ibid, p.141.
223   Ibid, p. 140.
224   Ibid, p. 141.

tax Nigerian women. Here's what followed: "On March 29 and 30, 1986, some 400 Bonny Island residents, including oil workers, shut down Africa's largest oil export terminal, claiming that the operator, Shell, had disrupted their lives and contributed nothing. Some 100 women sat on the Shell helipad to prevent any helicopter from landing at the tank farm base."[225]

After so many years of the oil companies' occupations, the people were finally rising up. Five thousand villagers held forty staff members of Shell hostage, protesting twenty-eight years of neglect. "The demonstrating women were estimated to be about 10,000 strong. The throng was made up of all age groups of women, including the very old."[226]

But the tides turned in the 1990s. Nigerian authorities covered up an October 1990 massacre of eighty unarmed villagers protesting Royal Dutch Shell. Even with this level of repression, over 100,000 Ogoni women and men gathered together for a daylong demonstration in January 1993. This massive mobilization flowed from the wellspring of the eighties uprisings initiated by oil belt women. Turner and Oshare point to a swell of positive results despite so much devastation:

Industrialization led to land alienation which motivated women's fight back. It elevated women's political impact by offering them vulnerable oil industry targets against which to concentrate their collective social power. It prompted feminist militancy which reforged the reciprocity between women and men, but this time on the new basis of class solidarity. Out of this experience is emerging a new society with the force and reason of

225 *Ibid*, p. 145.
226 *Ibid*, p. 147.

women, and their organization and consciousness at its forefront.[227]

WOMEN'S RESISTANCE IN AFRICA
BIRTHING A MOVEMENT IN JAMAICA

Rastafari has a deep well of connection to women and the fight against colonialism in Africa. The first mansion of Rastafari was named the Order of Nyahbinghi. Haile Selassie I was purportedly named the head of this order at a meeting of the Pan-African Congress in 1930. The word "Nyahbinghi" refers to both a singular figure and a popular movement in Africa, which became known to the Europeans in the late 1800s. In the early 1900s the movement was the driving force of the resistance against British colonialism in Uganda, the Germans in Rwanda, and the Belgians in the Congo. "The Nyabingi movement, influential in southwestern Uganda, was centered around a woman healer, Muhumusa, who was possessed by the spirit of Nyabingi, a legendary 'Amazon Queen.' Muhumusa organized armed resistance against German colonialists and was subsequently detained by the British in Kampala, Uganda, from 1913 to her death in 1945."[228]

According to Robert Rotberg's *Rebellion in Black Africa*, this women-centered popular movement "succeeded in immobilizing the administrative efforts of three colonial powers for nearly two decades, until its final suppression in 1928."[229] Nigeria was represented at the Pan-African Congress, although they were still colonized by the British. There are few public sources mentioning this historic meeting other than a 1935 article published in the *Jamaican Times*, which

---

227 *Ibid*, p. 160.

228 *Ibid*, pgs. 22–23.

229 Robert L. Rotberg, *Rebellion in Black Africa* (Oxford University Press, 1971), p. 60.

was quoted in the 1960 "University Report on the Rastafari Movement" by the University of the West Indies, and was the first real documentation of the movement.

The decline of resistance, which came with the demise of the movement in Uganda and Rwanda in the late 1920s, mirrors what happened in Nigeria and all over the colonial world. The cause of this finality bears consideration: the absence of the self-determination actively exemplified by Rastafari people. A significant dynamic contributing to the decline of Nyabingi in Uganda and Rwanda in the late twenties "was the increasing incorporation of local Africans into the colonial administrative structure and into the local mission hierarchies. Through recruitment into these organizations, Africans were also absorbed into the underlying incentive system of the colonial power."[230]

Widening the class divide (due to outside intervention) and forcing people to conform only promotes unrest among the disenfranchised—that is no way forward. This is a subject that appears frequently in reggae songs inspired by the Rastafari movement.

STRUCTURAL ADJUSTMENT IN CUBA AND PEAK OIL

Jamaica's neighboring island Cuba had a remarkable response to their own economic crisis. In Cuba, the government dealt with its own form of structural adjustment, although theirs was self-imposed. The fall of the Soviet Union created an economic crisis in Cuba in the 1990s, because the island nation was largely dependent on trade with Russia. It experienced a loss of 80 percent of their export market and 80 percent of their imports, including food, medicine, and oil.

---

230 Robert L. Rotberg, *Rebellion in Black Africa* (Oxford University Press, 1971), p. 131.

This challenge was to profoundly transform their economy. While places like Nigeria were forced to restructure their industries to primarily benefit the upper class and the foreign corporations, "the Cuban adjustment was designed to protect the standard of living of the Cuban masses and to preserve the social and economic gains of the Cuban Revolution, giving priority to the maintenance of the system of health, education and social security."[231] Cubans actively sought citizen participation by having consultations with organizations of workers, peasants, students, women, and their revolutionary committees. As they decentralized their government-owned enterprises, they encouraged the formation of co-ops for the people instead of letting international corporations privatize their economy.

The transition toward a sustainable economy was not an easy one. With the absence of oil, transportation was essentially halted; the average Cuban reportedly lost thirty pounds. "There were great shortages, but not starvation; unemployment, but not alienation; there were tensions, but not uprisings, much less generalized repression, as would have been normal in the rest of the world. In the worst moments, the health system was maintained and the schools continued functioning with used books, paper and pencils."[232]

The need to produce food locally, and the lack of chemical imports, meant the island had to develop systems to support organic agriculture. "In turning to gardening, individuals and neighborhood organizations took the initiative by identifying idle land in [Havana], cleaning it up and plant-

---

231 Charles McKelvey, "The Cuban Structural Adjustment Plan," *The View from the South: Commentaries on World Events from the Third World Perspective* (Global Learning, 2016).

232 *Ibid.*

ing."[233] Initiating this development in 1993, just a year before the final arrest of Ken Saro-Wiwa, the Cuban government awarded a $26,000 grant to a group of Australian permaculturalists to set up what would become the first permaculture demonstration project. Later, an urban permaculture center was established in Havana to continue educating people on the practice.

In 2006, Megan Quinn reported on an engineer-turned-farmer who was raising food for his neighborhood on his rooftop.

> On just a few hundred square feet he has rabbits and hens and many large pots of plants. Running free on the floor are gerbils, which eat the waste from the rabbits, and become an important protein source themselves. "Things are changing," Sanchez [the urban farmer] said. "It's a local economy. In other places people don't know their neighbors. They don't know their names. People don't say hello to each other. Not here."[234]

Previously focused on plantation agriculture, the island nation now had to turn away from tractors and turn to oxen, from exporting big mono-crops and spraying chemical pesticides on a large scale to following natural cycles and encouraging biodiversity. They were converting former plantations into organic production centers and trying to connect directly to markets in the US.

Cubans also employed ride-sharing as another community-based solution to deal with scarce resources. "In an

233 Megan Quinn, "The Power of Community: How Cuba Survived Peak Oil," *Permaculture Activist*, February 25, 2006.

234 *Ibid.*

inventive approach, virtually every form of vehicle, large and small, was used to build this mass transit system. Commuters ride in handmade wheelbarrows, buses, other motorized transport and animal-powered vehicles," Quinn writes.[235] Carlos Alzugaray, the former Cuban ambassador to the EU and minister-councilor to the Cuban embassy in Ethiopia, put it this way when we met with him at an accounting co-op in Havana: "When it came to the US and Cuba, it was like what Roberta Flack sang in 'Killing Me Softly.' But we Cubans ended up more like Gloria Gaynor's sentiments in her disco hit 'I Will Survive'!"

Chris Maher from the National Co+op Grocers board, who was also on my trip to Cuba, participated in a panel discussion with Cuban construction and textile co-op representatives. Maher represented consumer co-ops, which Cuba lacked, so together we advocated for the community-owned model. We met with a couple of economics professors from the University of Havana who were interested in starting one. At the time, however, it was not possible under the existing laws to enact a consumer co-op. But one thing was clear from all our discussions: co-ops in the US benefit tremendously from our national organizations like the NCG and the NCBA. Cuban co-ops would do well to form an organization that could advocate on their behalf.

Meanwhile, the US has a lot to learn from the Cuban people, not to mention the Ogoni people in Nigeria. Megan Quinn addresses this point succinctly:

> From the Community Solution's viewpoint, Cuba did what it could to survive, despite its ideology of a central-

---

235 Ibid.

ized economy [at the time]. In the face of peak oil and declining oil production, will America do what it takes to survive, in spite of its ideology of individualism and consumerism? Will Americans come together in community, as Cubans did, in the spirit of sacrifice and mutual support?

As the US government and its corporate allies now face the unification of Native American leadership, the Black Lives Matter movement, and white leftists resisting the Dakota Access Pipeline, people should remember George Jackson's warnings about fascism. The recent conflict in North Dakota is a blatant example of police forces serving and protecting an oil corporation against the will of the people, meting out legal violence against the original inhabitants of the land. This tendency absolutely reeks of a corporate-minded government and a recolonization of America.

As politicians continue to vie for such neocolonialist control, people need to rise up together with an informed perspective that honors all religions, just as Haile Selassie I espoused. He said we must cultivate "the ability to transcend narrow passions and to engage in honest conversation; for civilization is by nature 'the victory of persuasion over force.' Unity is strength."[236]

In Nigeria the government made tampering with a pipeline a crime punishable by death. And in Saro-Wiwa's case, merely speaking out against the injustice cost him his life.

KEN'S LAST WORDS

In Nigeria, the government and military acted as appendages

---

236 Haile Selassie I, *Selected Speeches of His Imperial Majesty Haile Selassie I* (One Drop Books, 2000), p. 22.

of the oil companies; similar to the US, where the CEO of Exxon is now the secretary of state, the oil companies put the leaders into power. This is the climate that led to the execution of Ken Saro-Wiwa. In his closing statement to the Nigerian military appointed tribunal, Saro-Wiwa was somewhat foreboding, although he expressed confidence that his cause would be vindicated. He said, "I predict that the scene here will be played and replayed by generations yet unborn. Some have already cast themselves in the role of villains, some are tragic victims, some still have a chance to redeem themselves. The choice is for each individual." He concluded by quoting the Holy Quran: "*All those that fight when oppressed incur no guilt, but Allah shall punish the oppressor. Come the day.*"

CHAPTER 9

SWEET SOMALIA

Oh, sweet Somalia,
Mogadishu never looked so bleak.
How could they mistreat Somalia?
Imports of bombs and foreign fighters kill the meek.

In a war-torn and desperate Somalia
Hungry pirates never miss a beat,
With American bombs on Somalia,
The cries of Muslim children fill the streets.

The Horn of Africa is an important place for human
   history,
And there came an ancient promise from Ashama, the
   Negus of Axum.
To the early followers of Muhammad, peace be upon
   him,
This was the first Christian nation and Muslims were
   free.

Islam came to Africa in the time of the Prophet,
Not with the sword, but with the surahs they saw fit,
To offer the Truth, that they were not a rival.
The Light from the Quran is the same Light from the
   Bible.

Oh, sweet Somalia.

They said he died, but they lied; always Selassie I abides.
They took the public for a ride but justice won't be denied.
DC denies they provide the guns to every side

And then broadcast worldwide; diplomacy is their guide.
You will find you got the rind when you signed on that
  line,
When you finished the deal they got the fruit, you got the
  peel.

In the previous chapters I have explored how the Rastafari movement helped shape my perspective on rebellion. In this same vein I will now examine Somalia. Within Somalia, I see the world—not just its war, but also its richness and resilience. Somalia is a society constantly coaxed into chaos by outside forces that have already mercilessly stripped away so many resources. As the coastal region in the Horn of Africa that is considered the birthplace of humanity, Somalia's ancient history is relevant to all of us, and thus is the crux of this book, which attempts to reconnect our histories in a principled way, without homogenizing them. After all, as Haile Selassie said, "Education is not an end in itself, but an aid to assist you to distinguish between good and evil, between the harmful and the useful."[237]

In recent years, Somalia has reentered the mainstream consciousness due to the media's sensationalistic coverage of Somalian "pirates." There have also been two somewhat recent major motion pictures set in Somalia, *Captain Phillips* starring Tom Hanks, and *Black Hawk Down*. The latter portrayed dramatic and familiar situations: brutal warlords battling heroic US soldiers trying to save thousands of starving innocents. It failed to mention, however, how the US helped create the chaos and starvation they were fighting by supporting a brutal dictator who capitalized on clan rivalries and slaughtered tens of thousands of his own people. Similarly,

---

237   H.I.H. Prince Ermias Sahle Selassie, *The Wise Mind of H.I.M. Emperor Haile Selassie I* (Frontline Books, 2004), p. 49.

Captain Phillips failed to give a backstory that truly provides a context for overstanding Somalian history, its pluralistic nature, and the decimation it has endured over and over due to colonial powers.

> *In the midst of the strife and turmoil which marks Africa today, the African peoples still extend the hand of friendship. But it is extended to those who desire the progress and the political and economic freedom of the African people, who are willing generously and without thought of selfish gain to assist us to our feet that We may stand by their side as brothers.*
> —Haile Selassie I, 1960[238]

Somalia is where a deep wellspring of history sprouted, where different cultures worked together to form a unified community, just like in Islamic Spain leading up to Europe's Renaissance. Rastafari people also embody this kind of incorporative, transformational orientation. Jake Homiak elaborates on this, emphasizing the "decentralizing and shifting demography of Rastafari," where those involved "develop their own social location within." He calls the movement "polycephalous" and an "interpretive community," having an "extreme multivocality and diffuse spatiality." He also says that "the movement was, in certain ways, international from its genesis and prefigured a postmodern geography of identity that exists *here* and *there* simultaneously."[239] Homiak helps

---

238 Haile Selassie I, *Selected Speeches of His Imperial Majesty Haile Selassie I* (One Drop Books, 2000), p. 206.

239 John Homiak, "When Goldilocks Met the Dreadlocks: Reflections on the Contributions of Carole D. Yawney to Rastafari Studies," *Let Us Start With Africa: Foundations of Rastafari Scholarship,* edited by Jahlani Niaah and Erin MacLeod (University of the West Indies Press, 2013), pgs. 59, 63, 65, and 67.

explain how Africa can be the focal point of an American perspective and how ancient history can retain relevance as we follow current events. This is why "Mortimo Planno and others have applied the oxymoronic label of 'the modern antique' to Rastafari."[240]

Carole D. Yawney's work centered on this pivotal figure—Mortimo Planno—who was the Rasta seen in newsreels calming the crowd down from Haile Selassie I's plane when he landed in Jamaica in 1966. Homiak writes, "[Yawney] had aligned herself with a strongly pan-Africanist orientation within Rastafari—one that placed more emphasis on finding ways to 'bridge the gap to Africa' than on the preoccupation with compliance with social codes."[241]

In *Rasta and Resistance*, Horace Campbell suggests that

> the body of ideas and beliefs which guided Rastafari [in the late 1950s] was deeper than simply a deification and glorification of Haile Selassie I. His Imperial Majesty (H.I.M.) stood for African independence in an uncompromising manner and the existence of Ethiopian Orthodoxy enabled Rastas to speak of the divinity of Haile Selassie, a conception quite consistent with the Coptic [beliefs].[242]

Campbell goes on to say that the Jamaican ruling class promoted studies that "centralized the personality of Haile Selassie I" in order to manipulate the movement. "Young Rastas, who were not aware of the links between Rasta and

---

240 *Ibid*, p. 74.

241 *Ibid*, p. 81.

242 Horace Campbell, *Rasta and Resistance: From Marcus Garvey to Walter Rodney* (Africa World Press, 1987), p. 102.

the international struggle against fascism in 1935, began to speak of Haile Selassie in terms of the Christian concept of God." Elder Rastas, Campbell continues, "felt that the church was within their body," but the state was successful in their "attempt to isolate the black nationalist thrust of Rasta by forcing it into a religious mold." This "increased with the intrusion of anthropologists and sociologists, who referred to Rasta as members of a 'messianic cult' . . ." As a whole, "The movement was denigrated until Walter Rodney brought new meaning and purpose to the understanding of the Rasta," from a scholarly perspective.[243]

Mortimo Planno was the chairman of the Ethiopian World Federation Local 37, an organization formed by a personal representative of Haile Selassie I. Yawney worked as Planno's recording secretary and was able to occupy a rare space for a white woman at the time. She participated in countless reasoning sessions between Rastas in the yards in and around Kingston.

Homiak identifies Planno as "a different kind of Dread," explaining,

> During the 1970s and 1980s, this phrase was frequently used by Rastafari to signal the level of individualism that existed within the movement with each brethren being accorded the freedom, within certain limits, to establish their own orientation in the culture. Planno clearly had an ability to stretch those limits.[244]

---

243 Ibid, pgs. 127–128.

244 John Homiak, "When Goldilocks Met the Dreadlocks: Reflections on the Contributions of Carole D. Yawney to Rastafari Studies," *Let Us Start With Africa: Foundations of Rastafari Scholarship*, edited by Jahlani Niaah and Erin MacLeod (University of the West Indies Press, 2013), pgs. 79 and 108–109.

As far as the consciousness that existed among the larger body of sistren and brethren, Homiak detects a determining principle:

> *The unity posited by the Rastafari can only arise out of an underlying tension and "argument" that is resolved in principle among specific participants, each of whom understand their own social and historic locations ([i.e.,] white Europeans, Afro-Caribbeans) . . . The process of argument, as in reasoning, was linked directly to the transcendent value that Rastafari place on a collective quest for oneness.[245]*

Haile Selassie I, the ever-guiding light of the movement and untiring champion of diplomacy, echoed this sentiment: "To meet together, to take council with one another, and to act in mutual cooperation, has proved a most fruitful method both in the secular and spiritual fields. Henceforth the way is open for you to follow this fruitful path . . ."[246]

Dr. Francis Deng was the first ambassador from Sudan to the United Nations, as well as their ambassador to Canada, Denmark, Finland, Norway, Sweden, and the US. When I met with Dr. Deng, he was an under-secretary general of the UN and the Special Advisor for the Prevention of Genocide. A group of Rastas and I sat in his Manhattan office after his son had come to our Rastafari Ancient Living Arts and Kulture Festival in North Carolina. Dr. Deng told us that his son was experiencing an existential crisis and that his interest in Rastafari had become quite helpful. He also reminded us

---

245   *Ibid*, p. 87.

246   H.I.H. Prince Ermias Sahle Selassie, *The Wise Mind of H.I.M. Emperor Haile Sellassie I* (Frontline Books, 2004), p. 91.

that Rastafari was the fastest-growing religion in Africa; he wanted to learn more about it. Our group reasoned with him for several hours.

RASTAFARI IN AFRICA

Rastafari's most obvious foothold in Africa is in Shashemane, Ethiopia. Shashemane sits on land Haile Selassie I granted to those who wished to return to their motherland. The grant was given from Haile Selassie I's private land holdings and was administered by the Ethiopian World Federation. Rastafarians were the only significant group to respond, yet their current state there is somewhat problematic. Once Haile Selassie I was overthrown, many in the government did not want to have a constant reminder of the monarchy a mere 150 miles from the capital, Addis Ababa. For this reason, it has been challenging for the settlers to be granted Ethiopian citizenship. Without citizenship they cannot own property, acquire building permits, and are lacking many other rights as well.

Shashemane may end up becoming a pilgrimage site for Rastas all over the world, but it remains to be seen if the current government will continue to tolerate them. The World Bank and the IMF have gained a lot of power in Ethiopia since the revolutionary government was overthrown, and this development, I believe, goes against everything Haile Selassie I stood for. "Aid," he said, "must be without strings . . . It is possible to influence positions and oblige adherence to this or that policy by economic pressure, but only at the expense of the pride and dignity of those who thus renounce their birthright as free men, and the bill of sale carries the caveat: 'revokable at will.'"[247]

---

247   Haile Selassie I, *Selected Speeches of His Imperial Majesty Haile Selassie I* (One Drop Books, 2000), p. 226.

The growth of Addis Ababa has caused quite a stir with populations at risk of losing their land, particularly the Oromo people, and Shashemane could fall to the same expansionist tendencies. The rapid growth of the Ethiopian economy has led to an unequal distribution of wealth and power, in typical World Bank and IMF fashion. Some encouraging signs suggest Rastas might be accepted, but it will likely take outside pressure to help make it happen.

Meanwhile, as Tom Freston wrote in *Vanity Fair* in 2014, the repatriates didn't exactly "get the welcome home they thought they deserved. They came, however, to create a perfect spiritual community, not to fit into Ethiopian society."[248] Even though the article states that the "Back to Africa movement never really happened," I would argue Rastafari *did* go home, as Dr. Francis Deng asserts. The *Vanity Fair* article also states, "You do not have to look far in Africa to see the influence of reggae music." But it is important to note that many Rastas don't see physical repatriation as a priority. Majek Fashek, a reggae musician from Nigeria, famously sang, "The promised land is not Africa, the promised land is a state of mind." This sentiment is fairly profound coming from an African artist.

After Bob Marley played a concert at Zimbabwe's Independence Day celebration in 1980, other reggae groups followed suit. According to Neil Savishinsky, "By the mid-1980s, as Fred Zindi reports, reggae had become such an integral part of the urban musical pop scene . . . one might have easily mistaken it for a local pop music genre."[249] Other aspects of Rasta culture also migrated, or repatriated. Some

---

248 Tom Freston, "The Promised Land," *Vanity Fair*, February 14, 2014.

249 Neil J. Savishinsky, "Transnational Popular Culture and the Global Spread of the Jamaican Rastafarian Movement," *New West Indian Guide* 68, No: 3/4, 1994, p. 268.

people have adopted the belief in Haile Selassie I's divinity and others haven't. Savishinsky explores this subject in depth:

> With the exception of a relatively small number of ortho-dox Rastas, Africans tend to downplay the importance of Haile Selassie, many refusing to accept the legitimacy of his divine status. The following statement by the Ivo-rian reggae star Alpha Blondy—who like many an African reggae artist is a self-proclaimed Rasta and ardent pan-Africanist—may best express the attitudes held by the majority of African Rastas toward this former Ethiopian monarch: "I, as an African Rasta, do not consider Selassie as being a living god. I consider him to be a symbol with a biblical background, like King Solomon and the Queen of Sheba as his ancestors. I believe in that. And I believe that he was the African who built the O.A.U. [Organization of African Unity], the first African consciousness of unity above political ideology and tribal consideration."[250]

Savishinsky further asserts that "the attraction of African youth to Rastafari may also be viewed as a direct outgrowth of their desire to participate in a contemporary international movement . . ."[251] Indeed, Rastafari has spread all over the continent, with a particularly strong foothold in South Africa. Midas Chawane from the University of Johannesburg asserts that reggae music, the primary vehicle of Rasta philosophy before South Africans could reason with Rasta elders or get their hands on any

250 *Ibid*, p. 278.
251 *Ibid*, p. 270.

relevant reading material, "was popular amongst freedom fighters (those involved in the struggle against apartheid), including those in exile and the township youth."[252]

Today, the movement has transitioned into a more formalized mansion structure after elders visited from various Rastafari mansions in Jamaica, including Binghi Irie Lion from the Nyahbinghi.

ASHAMA, THE NEGUS OF AXUM

Two early examples of culturally tolerant societies flourished in and around North Africa. One set the stage for the rich historical wellspring that would become the Ethiopian state, and the other, centered in Spain, spawned the Renaissance in Europe. In both cases, however, religious tolerance fell victim to outside aggression. But thankfully, Haile Selassie I carried these kinds of tolerant tendencies into the modern age: "Hence, if anybody says that differences exist between Moslems and Christians, that person is an enemy of Ethiopia."[253]

The capital of Axum was situated in the northern part of Ethiopia from the first century CE up until the end of the first millennium. The economy of Axum was largely fed by trade routes between Rome and India. King Ashama (also known as Ezana) converted to Christianity in the fourth century, making this the first Christian nation, although its biblical roots go back much further. Axum had a strong connection to the Old Testament because the Solomonic Dynasty had been set up there almost a thousand years before Christ.

Menelik I, the son of King Solomon and Makeda (or

---

252 Midas Chawane, "The Rastafari Movement in South Africa: Before and After Apartheid," *New Contree* No. 65, December 2012, p. 173.

253 Haile Selassie I, "Eritrea Hails Her Sovereign" (Imperial Ethiopian Government Press and Information Department, 1952).

Candace, the Queen of Sheba, as she's called in Acts in the Bible), was sent home to Ethiopia with Azuriah, the son of Zadok—Solomon's high priest. To his court, Solomon said, "Come, let us make him king of the country of Ethiopia, together with your children . . . Come, O ye councillors and officers, let us give [him] your firstborn children, and we shall have two kingdoms; I will rule here with you, and our children shall reign there."[254] Menelik and Zadok were accompanied by the firstborn sons of Israeli priests and officers, as well as the Ark of the Covenant itself. The Ethiopian Solomonic Dynasty preserved the Ark, along with Israel's traditions, when Solomon's reign crumbled. Israel then split apart and the Jews were carried away to captivity in Babylon.

In the third century, Mani, a Persian religious leader, considered Axum the third-largest power in the world, with Persia, Rome, and China first, second, and fourth, respectively. At its height, Axum's sphere of influence encompassed modern-day Ethiopia, Eritrea, Sudan, Egypt, Yemen, Saudi Arabia, and Somalia.

The history of ancient Ethiopia and the Horn of Africa begins at the dawn of human history itself. Axum had apparently been established by Ityoppis, the grandson of Ham and son of Cush. Richard Pankhurst, a British scholar whose mother was a friend to Haile Selassie I and a strong supporter of Ethiopia after Mussolini's invasion, lived in Ethiopia for over thirty years and was a professor of Ethiopian studies in the capital city. He discusses a Portuguese traveler who was the first European to write about the city in the sixteenth century and corroborated the legend that the Queen of Sheba lived there.[255] Pankhurst also reveals that, according

---

254 Sir E.A. Wallis Budge, *The Kebra Nagast* (Cosimo Classics 2004), p. 51.

255 Richard Pankhurst, *The Ethiopians: A History* (Wiley-Blackwell, 1998), p. 19.

to traditional Ethiopian lists of kings, "which are by no means necessarily reliable," there was an Axumite king "called Bazen, believed to have begun to reign eight years before the birth of Christ."[256]

Today, the Ethiopian government fights the so-called War on Terror by bombing Somalia on behalf of the US and engaging with the World Bank. My supposition is that if Haile Selassie was still reigning, or if a successor followed his lead, this would not be the case. A battle between the proponents of Christianity and Islam in this region flies in the face of an ancient promise made to the Prophet Muhammad (peace be upon him) by Ashama ibn Abjar, the Negus of Axum in 615 CE.

As king, Ashama was known for his piety. So when the Muslims were being persecuted in their homeland, the Prophet Muhammad (pbuh) told his people to go there, "to the land of Truth." Ashama and Muhammad (pbuh) had already exchanged brotherly communication, as it was acknowledged by both that Christianity and Islam shared the same source. At the inception of Islam was an Ethiopian named Bilal, one of the Prophet's most loyal companions, who was chosen to lead the call to prayer. David Robinson even claims that there was a "multicultural and multireligious identity at the heart of Ethiopia's history."[257] He devotes a whole chapter to this Christian nation in his 2004 book *Muslim Societies in African History*.

When the early Muslims reached Axum, they were challenged by the court as their pursuers had gotten there first and maligned the new religion to the king. In their defense,

---

256 *Ibid*, p. 22.

257 David Robinson, *Muslim Societies in African History* (Cambridge University Press, 2004), p. 109.

the Muslims simply read from the Holy Quran. After hearing verses from the Surah Mariam (the Virgin Mary), the Axumite king and many of the members of his court wept at its beauty. Because of the similarities they heard with their own faith, Ashama stated publicly that "the Light from the Quran is the same Light from the Bible," mirroring the statement above by Haile Selassie I. Ashama also declared that Muslims could live in Ethiopia for as long as they wished. This interaction is depicted in the 1976 movie *The Message*, starring Anthony Quinn.

THE "ORNAMENT OF THE WORLD"—ISLAMIC SPAIN

While Axum was still thriving, Europe, and more specifically Spain, had its own epoch of cultural tolerance. Unfortunately, any apparent appreciation for Islam seems to have gotten lost along the way, especially after the US-sponsored Afghan jihad against Russia in the 1970s. The extremist (or terrorist) forces we helped create then turned their sights on us, and in turn, the backlash has led many in the West to demonize a whole religion.

Back in the Middle Ages, the Islamic kingdom of Spain, known then as al-Andalus, wasn't as divisive as too many outsiders consider Islam to be today. Anyone who has actually lived amongst Muslims would know that terrorist groups like Isis don't come anywhere close to representing the majority. Nearly twenty million Shia Muslims from all over the region defied Isis by gathering in Iraq in November 2016, and in the wake of the 2015 terrorist attacks in Paris, seventy thousand Indian Sunni Muslim clerics issued a fatwa (a ruling on Islamic law) against terrorist groups like Isis, the Taliban, and Al-Qaeda, saying that they are not true Islamic organizations. In this vein, the rulers of al-Andalus demanded respect for the Jews and Christians who lived amongst them. They considered the followers of these religions the "Peoples of the Book," or *dhimmi* in Arabic. Maria Rosa Menocal, author of *Ornament of the World*, elaborates:

> *In principle, all Islamic polities were (and are) required by Quranic injunction not to harm the dhimmi, to tolerate the Christians and Jews living in their midst. But beyond that fundamental prescribed posture, al-Andalus was, from these beginnings, the site of memorable and distinctive interfaith relations. Here the Jewish community rose from the ashes of an abysmal existence under the Visgoths to the point that the emir who proclaimed himself caliph in the tenth century had a Jew as his foreign minister. Fruitful intermarriage among the various cultures and the quality of cultural relations with the dhimmi were vital aspects of Andalusian identity as it was cultivated over these first centuries.*[258]

In this environment of collaboration, the population produced unprecedented works of art, science, and literature. Jewish mysticism received the name *Kabbalah* and Sufi Muslims were free to dabble in their own brand of mysticism. This society, distinct from the caliphate centered in Baghdad, sprang from Damascus after a conflict between two family lines, subsequent to the passing of Prophet Muhammad (pbuh). The society they initiated in southern Europe lasted over seven hundred years and achieved incredible advancements in culture, mathematics, medicine, and astronomy. Mexican novelist Carlos Fuentes explains, "Muslim Spain

---

258 María Rosa Menocal, *The Ornament of the World* (Back Bay Books/, 2002), p. 30.

invented algebra, along with the concept of zero. Arabic numerals replaced the Roman system. Paper was introduced to Europe, as were cotton, rice, sugar cane, and the palm tree."[259] This society created astrolabes to navigate the stars. They developed telescopes, running water, aqueducts, avenues with shops, paved streets with lights, alchemy, chemistry, geometry, trigonometry, surgery, psychiatry, physiology, botany, geology, cosmogony, biology, sociology, architecture, and calligraphy.

It all began in 711 when Gibraltar (Gibr al-Tarik), a Berber chieftain, successfully invaded Spain, defeating the Goths, the Germanic invaders in the third century. The Goths had sacked Rome in 410 and then assumed power over most of the land and the peoples Rome had conquered. By taking Spain from the Goths, the North Africans were assuming land that the papacy had its eye on. It was the papacy's thirst for this kind of power that later added significance to the global colonial thrust by European nations, leading to the large-scale decimation of indigenous peoples in Africa and what we now call the Americas.

Skipping ahead, in 1455 Pope Nicholas V specifically issued the "Bull Romanus Pontifex," which served as one of the main influences for making war against nonbelievers and seizing their property:

> We bestow suitable favors and special graces on those Catholic kings and princes . . . athletes and intrepid champions of the Christian faith . . . to invade, search out, capture, vanquish, and subdue all Saracens and pagans whatsoever, and other enemies of Christ whereso-

---

259 Carlos Fuentes, *The Buried Mirror: Reflections on Spain and the New World* (Mariner Books/Houghton Mifflin Company, 1999), p. 53.

*ever placed, and . . . to reduce their persons to perpetual
slavery, and to apply appropriate . . . possessions, and
goods, and to convert them to . . . their use and profit.*[260]

Unfortunately, the fact that Muslims considered Jesus
their highest prophet seemed to be a fact lost on the pope,
who likely had sights on the wealth that could be gained
from the plunder. Regardless, the decree proved disastrous
for the Muslims who ruled the Mediterranean Sea and for
the people on Turtle Island (America). For the Africans, they
too would become a commodity traded across the seas, but the
foundation for this had been laid almost half a century earlier.

Beginning in 1418, the earliest colonial outposts established by the Portuguese, and then the Spanish, were sugar
plantations on the islands off the western coast of Africa.
This was apparently a consequence of the wealth generated by
al-Andalus and the production and consumption of sugar-
cane by the elite there. In turn, these Portuguese and Spanish traders institutionalized that African coast as the primary
source for slave labor. With this seemingly free labor force,
the national economies in southern Europe boomed, and the
plunder of those with whom the explorers came into contact
ensued.

In *Three American Empires,* John TePaske explains how
"the Mediterranean and not the European North is the
homeland of capitalism and of the Industrial Revolution. Italy,
southern France, Spain, and southern Germany witnessed
the rise of the first factories, the first banks and the first great
fairs."

---

260 Peter d'Errico, "Native Americans in America: A Theoretical and Historical
Overview," *Wicazo Sa Review* Vol. 14, No. 1 (Indigenous Resistance and Persistence,
1999), pgs. 7–28.

Because of various exports, including African slaves, Spain was a thriving center of commerce at the time Columbus first set sail across the great sea. Tellingly, regarding the true nature of capitalism, conquest and warfare were key aspects of the growth in prosperity.

> The nobility, partly organized into religious orders of monastic warriors, saw in warfare a ready source of ego enhancement and looted wealth. Its traditional ecominic interest lay in the extension of grazing range for its herds of cattle and sheep, coupled with a flourishing export trade in wool to northern Europe. The peasantry, on the other hand, consisted of soldier-cultivators, recruited into the army by promises and guarantees of freedom from servile encumbrances and charters of local self-rule. These peasants desired land, free land, to divide among their sons. In warfare, both nobility and peasantry gained their divergent ends.[261]

The Bishop Bartolome Las Casas of Spain, a famous missionary, recommended in 1517 the importation of Africans because the so-called "Indian" slaves were dying too quickly. 1492 was such a pivotal year for the world because not only had Europe made significant contact with the land across the sea, they had also successfully conquered the Islamic empire in Spain and expelled its Jewish inhabitants to solidify this dramatic Christian expansion of empire. Unfortunately, tolerance itself was conquered that year too.

Granada, the last Andalusian kingdom, was defeated in 1492. King Ferdinand and Queen Isabella, with the full

---

261 John J. TePaske, *Three American Empires*, Harper and Row, 1967.

power of the Catholic Church, carried out pogrom after pogrom. With the culture of tolerance eradicated, Muslims were forced to convert to Christianity. A harsh persecution followed. The reading of books in Arabic was prohibited and countless libraries and private collections were burned.

SOMALIA'S MARITIME HISTORY—PIRATES OR SURVIVORS?

> We Africans occupy a different—indeed a unique— position among the nations of this century. Having for so long known oppression, tyranny and subjugation, who, with better right, can claim for all the opportunity and the right to live and grow as freemen? Ourselves for long decades the victims of injustice, whose voices can be better raised in the demand for justice and right for all?[262]
> —Haile Selassie I

Only a few years after Ferdinand and Isabella captured Granada, Portuguese traders made contact with post-Axum Ethiopia. Axum's power as a political capital declined in the early 1100s CE, and the seat of power shifted to the south. After more than a century of domination by the mysterious Zagwe, the Solomonic Dynasty was restored in 1270 CE with Yekuno Amlak. This new ruler had close relations with the Islamic rulers of both Yemen and Egypt.

At the time Somalia was dominated by multiple empires, or sultanates, which effectively fought against the burning and looting by the Portuguese state. Meanwhile, trade with the Portuguese continued to grow. Under the Ajuran Sultanate the Somali maritime trade flourished, which enhanced

---

262 H.I.H. Prince Ermias Sahle Selassie, *The Wise Mind of H.I.M. Emperor Haile Sellassie I* (Frontline Books, 2004), p. 77.

relationships with North and East Africa, Arabia, India, Venetia, Persia, Egypt, Portugal, and China. The Warsangali Sultanate lasted for roughly the same period in the northeast and southeast of Somalia. At the end of their reign, they made treaties with the British when the so-called protectorate of British Somaliland was established. The Geledi Sultanate took over various land holdings of the Ajuran, and was later incorporated into Italian Somaliland. Their reign of power was far more brief, lasting from the late 1880s to 1910.

The Adal Sultanate was a multiethnic medieval Muslim state that flourished from around 1415 to 1577 CE. They controlled parts of Ethiopia, including Harar, Haile Selassie I's birthplace. The newly restored Solomonic Dynasty in Ethiopia, which continued from 1270 CE through colonial times, ended with Haile Selassie I's reign from 1930 to 1974. The line of Ethiopian emperors had varying degrees of peace and war with their Muslim neighbors, but the rich history of Axum's relationship with Islam set the stage for Yekuno Amlak to restart the dynasty with an eye toward diplomacy.

Somalia was established as an independent state in 1960, merging British and Italian Somalilands. Soon after, Mohamed Siad Barre, the army's commander, assumed power by waging a successful coup and declaring Somalia a Socialist state. He then quickly dissolved the Parliament and Supreme Court, and suspended the constitution. His penchant for enflaming clan rivalries to keep the heat off his rule ended up exploding into a civil war that ousted him in 1991. Meanwhile, his so-called Socialist state became a big concern in America's Cold War with Russia. Both sides were vying for influence in this strategic location. Russia poured arms into Somalia, exacerbating tensions surrounding Ethiopia's largely Somali-populated Ogaden region. Ethiopia, under Haile Selassie I, was the US's key ally in the Horn of Africa, so the US countered by giving the nation military assistance. But with Haile Selassie I's removal in 1974, the Soviets gained a stronger foothold there.

Siad Barre, with Italian military support, attacked Ethiopia in the aftermath of the Mengistu military coup. The transition in Ethiopia, from a monarchy with well-established traditions and complex international relationships, to a military junta dependent on Russia, created disarray. In an interesting turn of events, Russia financed five thousand Cuban troops to assist Ethiopia in defeating the invading Somali army. With the Soviets' new prominence in the region, the US moved to build relations with Siad Barre, even though he was commonly thought of as a dictator.

The US continued to support Barre and his murderous regime because it wanted a strategic military outpost close to the Persian Gulf. But when the US needed staging grounds for the 1990 war with Iraq, after that country's invasion of Kuwait, Saudi Arabia and other Gulf countries were willing to provide bases. Thus, the US's relationship with Siad Barre dissipated, which hastened the outbreak of the civil war that precipitated his ouster. General Mohammed Aideed soon rose to prominence (and served as the main antagonist in the movie *Black Hawk Down*).

I was living in DC when the two Black Hawk helicopters got shot down in a nation few Americans knew they were at war with. After seeing news footage showing General Aideed and other warlords engaging in internecine fighting, I played a show in downtown DC at the Black Cat club. As I approached the venue that evening, I looked over and saw the familiar Mogadishu Restaurant and could only wonder what the family who ran it were going through as their real history was being shortchanged in the slanderous media coverage. Few outlets considered the larger implications of US involvement and the despoliation of their seas by so many other countries. My newly piqued interest in the history of the region led me to dig deeper.

The Somalian "pirates" of recent history, who have been so easily demonized by media outlets, are fulfilling a need for commerce, which has been consistently stymied as the rich history of the region and the struggles of the inhabitants are ignored. So-called warlords, funded by various world powers in the interest of multinational corporations, continue to aggravate the situation. Mohamed Abdulkadir Ali fills in the blanks of Somalia's recent history:

> For over twenty years, Somalia's coastal waters have been the world's largest dumping ground for toxic waste and chemicals. EU firms have taken advantage of the country's descent into chaos to cheaply remove hazards, including nuclear waste, from Europe.
>
> Along the blue waters of the Indian Ocean, once home to thousands of species of fish, fishermen and their families die of malnutrition. There are no fish. European, Chinese and South Asian trawlers plunder Somalia's unprotected coastal waters, dramatically decreasing fish stock.
>
> Over two-thirds of young men and women in these villages have no jobs and live in abject poverty. Only a few miles away, cargo ships laden with hundreds of millions of dollars of goods and produce slowly slide by. This was the origin of piracy.[263]

---

263 Mohamed Abdulkadir Ali, "The Backstory of Somali Pirates Does Not Fit Neatly on the Big Screen," *Huffington Post*, November 2015, 2013.

Ali addresses a plain truth: these pirates are not "simple fisherman turned criminals." They're child soldiers, victimized by "ruthless warlords." The children are the "biggest victims of piracy," he says. With the widespread poverty and an unemployment rate of 67 percent, there are few opportunities for a sustainable livelihood.

Johann Hari provides a different perspective in a 2009 essay in the *Independent*, offering a fresh look at the history of piracy. "Pirates have never been quite who we think they are," he writes. He points to the "golden age of piracy," from 1650 to 1730, and suggests that the idea we have today about pirates like Bluebeard is the result of an effective propaganda campaign by the British government. He points out that "pirates were often saved from the gallows by supportive crowds . . . Why? What did they see that we can't?"

Merchant sailors and members of the British navy were worked to the bone. Johann Hari's article explains what came next:

> *Pirates were the first people to rebel against this world. They mutinied—and created a different way of working on the seas. Once they had a ship, the pirates elected their captains, and made all their decisions collectively, without torture. They shared their bounty out in what Rediker calls "one of the most egalitarian plans for the disposition of resources to be found anywhere in the eighteenth century."*
>
> *They even took in escaped African slaves and lived with them as equals.*[264]

---

264 Johann Hari, "You Are Being Lied to About Pirates," the *Independent* (UK), January 5, 2009.

Hari pivots to 1991, "when the government of Somalia collapsed. Its nine million people have been teetering on starvation ever since—and the ugliest forces in the Western world have seen this as a great opportunity to steal the country's food supply and dump our nuclear waste in their seas."[265]

In 2004, the Islamic Courts Union rose to prominence in Somalia and stabilized the country, even beginning peace talks with Sudan. But subversion by outside forces again weakened the region. This vacuum helped encourage the rise of Al-Shabaab, an ally to Al-Qaeda.

I bring up this history of regional degeneration in Somalia, juxtaposed with the history of cultural tolerance there and in Spain, for a very specific reason. We can't reliably form an analysis of what's going on today or work toward a better world unless we are willing to dig into the past, perhaps finding the pearls of wisdom among resistance movements contending with international and increasingly unregulated capitalistic empires. We are too easily goaded into reaction by international corporate forces that stem from an ancient past themselves, and yet we must resist the fascists and our own fascist tendencies at all costs.

---

265 *Ibid.*

AFTERWORD

In this book I have taken you through many subjects, hoping you will see certain connections across history and between nations. I've also woven together a proverbial quilt of icons. But this exercise hasn't been solely about bringing revolutionary figures into your life; I hope to encourage you to pinpoint your own role models based on what you've experienced and the kind of guidance you need. What does the quilt you've made for yourself look like? We all carry one, whether we realize it or not. What *should* it look like? Are there devious characters you have subconsciously picked up as guides leading you astray? Are core values holding you back? Are your icons turning into idols you can't challenge? I continue to ask myself these same questions.

In my view, extreme begets extreme. Far-left-leaning Yippies like Jerry Rubin in the 1960s, for example, beget the alt-right Milo Yiannopoulos in 2016. Rubin ended his career as a right-leaning commentator and I expect Yiannopoulos will complete a similar flip-flop. As the pendulum swings from the leftism of the sixties and seventies, how far right will it go? Think about that as it begins to swing back to the left, after the extremism of the Republican Tea Party has helped usher in the Trump presidency.

How many people are you willing to alienate as you push back against the fascists? Dishonest discourse is a waste of energy. The truth really does matter, and I believe it prevails in the end, no matter how hard some try to cloud it. The way forward is about inclusion, without whitewashing the stains from the past. It's about the principle of "unity without uniformity," as Jake Homiak declares in his work chronicling Rastafari history, and also the "principled unity" Dhoruba Bin Wahad so eloquently speaks of.

Venturing to Jamaica and Cuba in 2016, doing co-op work, certainly challenged *my* truths. Many ideas I had been tossing around in my head for years were finally put to the test. For instance, I found that cultural appropriation wasn't just about crossing the "race" divide, as I observed Jamaican society exploiting Rasta culture without ever giving Rasta communities their due.

I kept my own level of appropriation in check in my travels. I had recently cut my dreadlocks, which I have had off and on for almost thirty years. My habit has been to grow my locks for seven years at a time, mostly because it makes sense to keep myself fresh. Each time I shed them, I can renew my vow in a way that feels like I am moving forward. Since this is not in keeping with traditional Rasta practices, I have often felt at odds with some who haven't overstood. No matter; my aim is to live true to those who have taught me, without selling myself out in the process. After all, like you, I am a complex human being, and this leads to the final metaphor I will throw your way—ajiaco soup. This I found in Cuba.

SO MUCH MORE THAN A MELTING POT

Since America is often referred to as a melting pot, does this mean the country represents the hot metal around the ingredients that dissolves them into a homogenous sludge? Yikes! The Cuban anthropologist Fernando Ortiz deepened the concept by pointing to the complexities involved. Earlier in Cuban anthropological circles, his key development was to coin the term "Afro-Cuban" and to create a scholarly association devoted to digging into this new field of study. He challenged notions of acculturation by creating the concept of "transculturation."

The gist was that when two societies meet, rather than looking at appropriation as one group shedding their culture in order to adopt another, as in acculturation, transculturation acknowledges that "the process of cultural contact and change never moves in one direction only. Rather, all cultures in contact transform each other and create a new culture, different from the original ones."[266] Ortiz felt that this kind of transculturation happened on a wider scale in Cuba than anywhere else, and even though it defines "Cubanness," it happens "among all peoples," therefore it's applicable to any modern society. His description of the Cuban people's experience of intermixing, perhaps as a model for all nations, is certainly compelling. He said that their "loving embraces" have been "more frequent, more complex, more tolerated, and more prefigured of a universal peace among the bloods."[267]

João Felipe Goncalves, in his preface to Ortiz's *The Human Factors of Cubanidad*, provides context for Ortiz's thinking about transculturation, so we can better understand why a comparison to ajiaco soup is such a potent analogy to Cuban identity. "The ajiaco metaphor powerfully subverts an image that is found in several nationalistic discourses across the globe: that of 'roots,'" Goncalves writes. He calls out nationalists for using the term *roots* by highlighting Ortiz's

---

266 João Felipe Goncalves, "The Ajiaco in Cuba and Beyond" preface to "The Human Factors of Cubanidad" by Fernando Ortiz, HAU: *Journal of Ethnographic Theory*, 2014, p. 449.

267 Ibid, p. 463.

statement that "no one can claim roots in Cuba—not even indigenous peoples, who also came from somewhere else." Goncalves then provides specifics, identifying Spain's influence as a "cultural trunk." But like the Africans who were "uprooted and transplanted," none of these ethnic groups were ever "well-sowed in the island." Then he quotes Ortiz at length:

> We Cubans have a peculiar relation to our roots: we eat them. What is the ajiaco if not a root roast, a kind of funeral pyrex? You take your favorite aboriginal roots— malanga [yam], yucca, boniato—and you cook them until they are soft and savory. In keeping with your roots' roots, you might even cook them in a hole in the ground. But then you consume them. You don't freeze them. You don't preserve them. You don't put them in a root museum.[268]

There are important nuances in the way ajiaco soup is made. Ortiz made it clear that the soup is one that never stops being cooked, because additional ingredients are constantly added. In the quoted lecture, Ortiz was speaking at the University of Havana in 1939. As he intoned, race is "nothing but a civil status granted by anthropological authorities," and he challenged the oversimplified concept of the melting pot by anointing the now immortal ajiaco. He traced the origins of the stew to the Taino Indians, who "carried out the first revolution, that of establishing agriculture." He then related their stew to ones that all peoples have developed as a basis of survival:

---

268   *Ibid*, p. 451.

> *Into the pot went everything edible, the meats without cleaning and sometimes already rotting, the vegetables without peeling and often with worms that gave them more substance. Everything was cooked together and everything was seasoned with strong doses of chili pepper, doses that covered all of the unpleasantness through the supreme stimulant of their sting. From this pot one would take what one wanted to eat at the moment; the remainder would stay there for meals to come.*[269]

Adding new water, the cook would resume the process the next day. New ingredients would be added day after day, with the broth thickening with each different substance and flavor. Ortiz compelled his audience to follow the metaphor. He identified the open pot as Cuba, "placed in the fire of the tropics," and how the "lively fire of the flame and the slow fire of the embers" relate to the island nation's two seasons. Where one feeds from the pot also has implications. "Cubanidad," he explained, "has a different flavor and consistency depending on whether it is scooped from the bottom, from the fat belly of the pot, or from its mouth, where the vegetables are still raw and the clear broth bubbles."[270]

He then went into further detail about the particular ingredients, incorporating all peoples who have added a flavor or texture to the dish, none more valuable than the other. But when it comes to the name itself, Ortiz was explicit—ajiaco is "composed of a linguistic root of Black African origin," with a "Castilian ending that gives the word a pejorative tone, utterly appropriate for a conquistador facing a colonial

---

269   *Ibid*, p. 461.

270   *Ibid*, p. 463.

stew." The African root is used to name the indigenous plant of the Tainos, so the term itself profoundly relates to all three cultures.

Ever diligent, Ortiz also pointed out the disparate origins within the individual groups of people who settled, or were taken there, positing that the Tainos were perhaps "the most homogenous in their lineage." Because the Africans were forced there as slaves, their backgrounds were as varied as the many different climates and topographies of the continent itself. The African contingent, Ortiz held, was composed of "a multitude of origins, races, languages, cultures, classes, sexes, ages . . . like the canes, they were milled and squeezed so as to extract the juice of their labor."[271]

> *And what will one say of the Whites, now so vexed with each other over questions of race? . . . What will we say of these German, French, English, or Italian races, which do not exist except in fantasy of those who labor to convert a changeable concept of history into a hereditary and fatal criterion of biology?*[272]

Ortiz pointedly argued that people later known as "white" had been "dominated in their land" and then became "dominators in the land of others,"[273] which led to "the oppressed terrified by punishment, and the oppressor terrified by revenge."[274] He urges us to consider culture, not race, when we look at people—because different cultures exist within each "race."

---

271 *Ibid*, p. 472.
272 *Ibid*, p. 465.
273 *Ibid*, p. 471.
274 *Ibid*, p. 473.

Ortiz openly celebrated Afro-Caribbeans when explaining "Cubanidad." He not only made a nod to their labor—building up Cuba to the point where it could compete in the world's markets—but he also discussed Africans' contributions to art and culture. Like Rastafari itself, "Cubania," he wrote, "did not rain from above, it sprouted from below."[275]

As Haile Selassie I implored, "Do not fall into the narrowness which looks only to the borders of your nation . . . We must move ahead in concert with all mankind."[276] With cooperative economics, together we can build an inclusive future truly worth living.

---

275 Ibid, p. 478.

276 H.I.H. Prince Ermias Sahle Selassie, The Wise Mind of H.I.M. Emperor Haile Selassie I (Frontline Books, 2004), p. 87.

RASTAFARI HISTORICAL TIME LINE

1896—Under Menelik II, the Ethiopians defeated the Italians at Adowa. "Ethiopianism" emerged throughout Africa and the African diaspora.

1900—W.E.B. Du Bois and Dr. Robert Love organized the first Pan-African Conference.

1909—W.E.B. Du Bois formed the NAACP, and included Ethiopian history in his articles, speeches, plays, and poems.

1914—Marcus Garvey formed the Universal Negro Improvement Association and African Communities League in Jamaica, preaching messages such as "Back to Africa!" and "Africa for the Africans!"

1916—Garvey moved the UNIA to New York and eventually gained millions of members.

1919—Du Bois held the first Pan-African Congress in Paris, in conjunction with the Paris Peace Conference, sponsored by the European and American powers at the end of World War I.

1921—Jamaican Bedwardites launched a revivalist movement advocating for black nationalism, repatriation, and the coming of the returned Messiah from Africa.

1930—Ras Tafari was coronated "Haile Selassie I, Emperor of Ethiopia, King of Kings, Lord of Lords, Conquering Lion of the Tribe of Judah." Also coronated was his queen, Empress Menen I.

1931—Joseph Nathaniel Hibbert, president of the Costa Rican UNIA, returned to Jamaica praising Haile Selassie I as the Almighty God. He later established the Ethiopian Mystic Masons. Archibald Henry Dunkley was another influential preacher in the thirties who also proclaimed Haile Selassie I as Christ returned.

1932—Leonard Howell returned to Jamaica preaching the divinity of Haile Selassie I, encouraging Jamaicans to recognize him as their king instead of the king of England.

1935—Italian fascists invaded Ethiopia in the early stages of World War II.

1937—Dr. Malaku Bayen, a personal representative of Haile Selassie I, created the Ethiopian World Federation in New York.

1938—The first Jamaican branch of the Ethiopian World Federation opened.

1940—Leonard Howell formed a commune called Pinnacle in the St. Catherine Parish of Jamaica where thousands of Rastafari adherents grew ganja for meditation and produced crops such as peas, beans, yams, bananas, cassavas, corn, and coconuts for trade.

1941—Haile Selassie I expelled the Italians from Ethiopia with the aid of the British military.

1941–1944—The Youth Black Faith, which ultimately became the Nyahbinghi Order, originated in Trench Town, Jamaica, a region that established Rastafari cultural expressions such as dreadlocks, Ital diets (vegetarian, nonprocessed foods), and the use of ganja as a sacrament. Ras Boanerges, a founding member of the Nyahbinghi Order, regarded smoking ganja as a biblically condoned practice.

1948—Haile Selassie I gave five hundred acres of his private land to members of the Ethiopian World Federation as a Shashamane land grant. This land was designated for those in the diaspora who had helped the cause for Ethiopia's defense during the Italian occupation to return to Africa.

1954—Rastas were expelled from the Pinnacle commune and the community was permanently disbanded.

1958—Prince Emmanuel Charles Edwards established the Bobo Shanti Black International Congress Church in Spanish Town, Jamaica.

1960—The University of the West Indies assembled an official report documenting the shared beliefs among the Rastafari movement. This report prompted Caribbean governments to sponsor an African delegation to research the possibilities of Jamaican repatriation.

1961—The Jamaican government sent Rastafari brethren Mortimo Planno, Douglas Mack, and Filmore Alvarenga to Africa to meet with Haile Selassie I.

1963—Haile Selassie I formed the Organization of African Unity.

1966—Haile Selassie I visited Jamaica and met with Mortimo Planno, Joseph Nathaniel Hibbert, and Prince Emmanuel Edwards.

1968—Vernon Carrington, also called Prophet Gad, formed the Twelve Tribes of Israel branch of Rastafari in Kingston, Jamaica. Bob Marley, a member of the Twelve Tribes of Israel, subsequently globalized the Rastafari message.

BIBLIOGRAPHY

Alexander, Michelle. *The New Jim Crow: Mass Incarceration in the Age of Colorblindness*, The New Press, 2010.

Ali, Mohamed Abdulkadir. "The Backstory of Somali Pirates Does Not Fit Neatly on the Big Screen," *Huffington Post*, November 25, 2013.

Aristide, Jean-Bertrand. *In the Parish of the Poor: Writings from Haiti*, Orbis Books, 1990.

Ayele, Yelibenwork. "Slavery in Ethiopia," *African Holocaust*, October 25, 2011, http://africanholocaust.net/slavery-in-ethiopia/.

Bey, Hakim. *T.A.Z.: The Temporary Autonomous Zone, Ontological Anarchy, Poetic Terrorism*, Autonomedia, 1991.

Bisson, Terry. *On a Move: The Story of Mumia Abu-Jamal*, Litmus Books, 2000.

Brown, Stephen D. *Haunted Houses of Harpers Ferry: Regional Ghost Stories*, The Little Brown House, 1976.

Budge, Sir E.A. Wallis. *The Kebra Negast*, Cosimo Classics, 2004.

Campbell, Horace. *Rasta and Resistance: From Marcus Garvey to Walter Rodney*, Africa World Press, 1987.

Chawane, Midas. "The Rastafari Movement in South Africa: Before and After Apartheid," *New Contree* No. 65, December 2012, p. 173.

Cook, Roy. "Plains Indian View of the 'Buffalo' Soldier," *American Indian Source*, http://americanindiansource.com/buffalo%20soldiers/buffalosoldiers.html.

Cumbie, Patricia. "The Rochdale Pioneers' Message to the Future," CDS Consulting Co-op Library, January 30, 2009.

Daigh, Michael. *John Brown in Memory and Myth*, McFarland, 2015.

Dale, Richard. *Who Killed Sir Walter Ralegh?*, History Press, 2011.

Davidson, Basil. *The Lost Cities of Africa*, Back Bay Books/Little, Brown and Company, 1987.

Davis, Angela Y. "Political Prisoners, Prisons, and Black Liberation," *History Is a Weapon*, May 1971, http://www.historyisaweapon.com/defcon1/davispoprprblli.html.

Dembele, Demba Moussa. "The International Monetary Fund and World Bank in Africa: A 'disastrous' record," *Pambazuka News: Voices for Freedom and Justice*, September 23, 2004, https://www.pambazuka.org/governance/international-monetary-fund-and-world-bank-africa-disastrous-record.

d'Errico, Peter. "Native Americans in America: A Theoretical and Historical Overview," *Wicazo Sa Review* Vol. 14, No. 1, Indigenous Resistance and Persistence (Spring 1999): 7–28.

DeRoche, Andrew J. *Andrew Young: Civil Rights Ambassador*, Rowman & Littlefield, 2003.

Dohrn, Bernardine. "Homeland Imperialism: Fear and Resistance," *Monthly Review: An Independent Socialist Magazine*, Vol. 55, No. 3 (July–August 2003).

Dread, Doctor. *The Half That's Never Been Told: The Real-Life Reggae Adventures of Doctor Dread*, Akashic Books, 2015.

Dribben, Betsy. "Social Co-operatives and Prison Systems," *Co-op News*, November 12, 2015, https://www.thenews.coop/99345/sector/worker-coops/blog-social-co-operatives-prison systems/.

Du Bois, W. E. B. *John Brown*, G. W. Jacobs, 1909.

Dunbar-Ortiz, Roxanne. *An Indigenous Peoples' History of the United States*, Beacon Press, 2014.

Elijah, J. Soffiyah. "The Reality of Political Prisoners in the United States: What September 11 Taught Us About Defending Them," *Harvard BlackLetter Law Journal*, Vol. 18 (2002).

Fanon, Frantz. *Black Skin, White Masks*, Grove Press, 2008.

Freston, Tom. "The Promised Land," *Vanity Fair*, February 14, 2014, https://www.vanityfair.com/news/politics/2014/02/shashemane-ethiopia-rastafarian-utopia.

Friedmann, Alex. "Prison Privatization: The Bottom Line," CorpWatch.org, August 21, 1999, https://corpwatch.org/article/prison-privatization-bottom-line.

Fuentes, Carlos. *The Buried Mirror: Reflections on Spain and the New World*, Mariner Books/Houghton Mifflin Company, 1999.

George, Susan. *How the Other Half Dies: The Real Reasons for World Hunger*, Penguin Books, 1986.

Goitom, Hanibal. "Abolition of Slavery in Ethiopia," In Custodia Legis, Library of Congress, February 14, 2012, https://blogs.loc.gov/law/2012/02/abolition-of-slavery-in-ethiopia/.

Goncalves, João Felipe. "The Ajiaco in Cuba and Beyond" preface to

"The Human Factors of Cubanidad" by Fernando Ortiz, *HAU: Journal of Ethnographic Theory*, 2014,

Goodman, Jeff. "What a Prison Sentence Really Means," *Minneapolis Star Tribune*, December 30, 1998.

Gordon Nembhard, Jessica. *Collective Courage: A History of African American Cooperative Economic Thought and Practice*, Pennsylvania State University Press, 2014.

Haile-Selassie, Teferra. *The Ethiopian Revolution 1974–1991: From a Monarchical Autocracy to a Military Oligarchy*, Routledge, 1997.

Haiphong, Danny. "Why George Jackson Matters Through the Lens of Blood in My Eye," *Black Agenda Report*, September 9, 2015, https://blackagendareport.com/george_jackson_blood_in_my_eye.

Hari, Johann. "You Are Being Lied to About Pirates," *The Independent* (UK), January 5, 2009, https://www.independent.co.uk/voices/commentators/johann-hari/johannhari-you-are-being-lied-to-about-pirates-1225817.html.

Hattingh, Shawn. "A Shell of Democracy," May 25, 2007, *Royal Dutch Shell PLC*, http://royaldutchshellplc.com/2007/05/25/a-shell-of-democracy/.

Hausman, Gerald. *The Kebra Nagast: The Lost Bible of Rastafarian Wisdom and Faith from Ethiopia and Jamaica*, St. Martin's Press, 1997.

Henrichson, Christian and Ruth Delaney, "The Price of Prisons: What Incarceration Costs Taxpayers," Vera Institute of Justice, February 2012.

Homiak, John. "When Goldilocks Met the Dreadlocks: Reflections on the Contributions of Carole D. Yawney to Rastafari Studies," *Let Us Start With Africa: Foundations of Rastafari Scholarship*, edited by Jahlani Niaah and Erin MacLeod, University of the West Indies Press, 2013.

Horwitz, Tony. *A Voyage Long and Strange: Rediscovering the New World*, Picador/Henry Holt and Co., 2008.

Houston, Drusilla Dunjee. *Wonderful Ethiopians of the Ancient Cushite Empire*, Peggy Bertram Publishing, 2007.

Ifateyo, Ajowa Nzinga. "The World's First Prisoner Worker Co-op: Transforming Prisoners' Lives Through Cooperation in Puerto Rico," *Grassroots Economic Organizing*, September 16, 2015, http://www.geo.coop/story/worlds-first-prisoner-worker-co-op.

Ignatiev, Noel. *Treason to Whiteness Is Loyalty to Humanity: An Inter-*

view with Noel Ignatiev of Race Traitor magazine, excerpted from the anarchist tabloid THE BLAST! (June/July 1994), http://nypolisci.org/files/poli15/Readings/Treason%20to%20 Whiteness.pdf.

Intergaláctico, El Kilombo. Beyond Resistance: Everything. An Interview with Subcomandante Insurgente Marcos, PaperBoat Press, 2008.

Jackson, George L. Blood in My Eye, Black Classic Press, 1996.

Jackson, John G. Ages of Gold and Silver and Other Short Sketches of Human History, American Atheist Press, 1990.

James, C.L.R. A New Notion: Two Works by C.L.R. James, PM Press, 2010.

James, Joy (Editor). Warfare in the American Homeland: Policing and Prison in a Penal Democracy, Duke University Press, 2007.

Josephy Jr., Alvin M. 500 Nations: An Illustrated History of North American Indians, Knopf, 1994.

Kapuściński, Ryszard. The Emperor: Downfall of an Autocrat, Vintage Books, 1989.

Katz, Sandor Ellix. Wild Fermentation: The Flavor, Nutrition, and Craft of Live-Culture Foods, Chelsea Green Publishing, 2003.

Kerness, Bonnie and Sundiata Acoli, "Effects and Use of Control Units," April 1996, http://www.sundiataacoli.org/effects-and-uses-of-control-units-22.

Ki-Zerbo, Joseph (Editor). UNESCO General History of Africa, Vol. 1, Abridged Edition: Methodology and African Prehistory, University of California Press, 1989.

Klein, Naomi. The Shock Doctrine: The Rise of Disaster Capitalism, Picador, 2008.

Kinsman, Gary. "The Politics of Revolution: Learning from Autonomist Marxism," El Kilombo, http://www.elkilombo.org/the-politics-of-revolution-learning-from-autonomist-marxism/.

Lazare, Sarah. "What You Need to Know About the DOJ's Claim It Is Ending Private Prisons," AlterNet, August 18, 2016, https://www.alternet.org/civil-liberties/what-you-need-know-about-dojs-claim-it-ending-private-prisons.

Lee, Butch and Red Rover. Night-Vision: Illuminating War and Class on the Neo-Colonial Terrain, AK Press, 1998.

Lifshitz, Fima. An African Journey Through Its Art, AuthorHouse, 2009.

Malam, John. Exploring Ancient Egypt, Evans Brothers, 1997.

Mann, Charles C. *1491: New Revelations of the Americas Before Colum-bus*, Vintage Books, 2011.

Mann, Eric. *Comrade George: An Investigation into the Life, Political Thought, and Assassination of George Jackson*, Harper & Row, 1974.

Mansingh, Ajai and Laxmi. "Hindu Influences on Rastafarianism," in Rex Nettleford, ed., *Caribbean Quarterly Monograph: Rasta-fari* (Kingston: Caribbean Quarterly, University of West Indies, 1985).

McDade, Jesse N. *Frantz Fanon: The Ethical Justification of Revolution*, Boston University, 1970.

McHenry, Keith. *Hungry For Peace: How You Can Help End Poverty and War with Food Not Bombs*, See Sharp Press, 2012.

McKelvey, Charles. "The Cuban Structural Adjustment Plan," *Global Learning*, September 20, 2016, http://www.globallearning-cuba.com/blog-umlthe-view-from-the-southuml/the-cuban-structural-adjustment-plan.

McPherson, E.S.P. *The Culture-History and Universal Spread of Rasta-fari: Two Essays*, Black International Iyahbinghi Press, 1993.

Menocal, María Rosa. *The Ornament of the World: How Muslims, Jews, and Christians Created a Culture of Tolerance in Medieval Spain*, Back Bay Books/Little, Brown and Company, 2002.

Merchant, Carolyn. *The Death of Nature: Women, Ecology and the Sci-entific Revolution*, HarperOne, 1990.

Mintz, Sidney W. *Sweetness and Power: The Place of Sugar in Modern History*, Viking Penguin Inc., 1985.

Moriarty, Meegan. "From Bars to Freedom: Prisoner Co-ops Boost Employment, Self-Esteem and Support Re-Entry into Society," *Rural Cooperatives*, January/February 2016.

Oates, Stephen B. *To Purge This Land with Blood: A Biography of John Brown*, University of Massachusetts Press, 1984.

Owens, Joseph. *Dread: The Rastafarians of Jamaica*, Heinemann, 1982.

Pankhurst, Richard. *The Ethiopians: A History*, Wiley-Blackwell, 1998.

Piette, Betsey. "Supreme Court Denies Mumia Right to Present New Witnesses," *Workers World*, October 18, 2008, https://www.work-ers.org/2008/us/mumia_1023/.

Quinn, Megan. "The Power of Community: How Cuba Survived Peak Oil," *Permaculture Activist*, February 25, 2006, https://www.resilience.org/stories/2006-02-25/power-community-how-cuba-survived-peak-oil/.

Reynolds, David S. *John Brown, Abolitionist: The Man Who Killed Slavery, Sparked the Civil War, and Seeded Civil Rights*, Alfred A. Knopf, 2005.

Robinson, David. *Muslim Societies in African History*, Cambridge University Press, 2004.

Rodney, Walter. *How Europe Underdeveloped Africa*, Bogle-L'Ouverture Publications, 1972.

Rogers, J.A. *Nature Knows No Color-Line*, Helga M. Rogers, 1952.

Roosevelt, Elliott. *F.D.R.: His Personal Letters, 1928–1945*, Duell, Sloan and Pearce, 1950.

Rotberg, Robert L. *Rebellion in Black Africa*, Oxford University Press, 1971.

Sanchez, Pedro. "Interview with Ramona Africa One MOVE," *Prison News Service* #55, October 1996, http://www.hartford-hwp.com/archives/45a/115.html.

Saro-Wiwa, Ken. *A Month and a Day: A Detention Diary*, Penguin Books, 1995.

Savishinsky, Neil J. "Transnational Popular Culture and the Global Spread of the Jamaican Rastafarian Movement," *New West Indian Guide/Nieuwe West-Indische Gids*, Vol. 68, No. 3/4 (1994).

Schlosser, Eric. "The Prison-Industrial Complex," *Atlantic*, December 1998, https://www.theatlantic.com/magazine/archive/1998/12/the-prison-industrial-complex/304669/.

Selassie, H.I.H. Prince Ermias Sahle. *The Wise Mind of H.I.M. Emperor Haile Sellassie I*, Frontline Books, 2004.

Selassie I, Haile. *Selected Speeches of His Imperial Majesty Haile Selassie I*, One Drop Books, 2000.

Selassie I, Haile. *Important Utterances of H.I.M. Emperor Haile Selassie I*, One Drop Books, 2000.

Selassie I, Haile. "Eritrea Hails Her Sovereign," Imperial Ethiopian Government Press and Information Department, 1952.

Selassie I, Haile. *The Autobiography of Emperor Haile Selassie I: King of Kings of All Ethiopia and Lord of Lords, My Life and Ethiopia's Progress Volume II: Addis Ababa 1996*, Frontline Books, 1999.

Shakur, Assata, Mumia Abu-Jamal, and Dhoruba Bin Wahad. *Still Black, Still Strong: Survivors of the War Against Black Revolutionaries*, Semiotext(e), 1993.

Shalhoup, Mara. "As American As Cherry Pie," *Creative Loafing Atlanta*, January 23, 2002.

Singleton, Aakhun George W. *Esoteric Atannuology, Egyptology and Rastafariology, Volume I,* Enlightenment Publications, 1997.

Slade, André M. and Katarína Križáni. *Where to from Here: Cognition,* Xlibris, 2014.

Sonnie, Amy and James Tracy. *Hillbilly Nationalists, Urban Race Rebels, and Black Power,* Melville House, 2011.

Starkey, Brando Simeo. *In Defense of Uncle Tom: Why Blacks Must Police Racial Loyalty,* Cambridge University Press, 2015.

Steffens, Roger. "Rastas of the Canyon: Take a Trip to the Indian Reservation Where Bob Marley and Reggae Music Reign Supreme," *High Times,* February 1993.

Stephens, Gregory. "A Second Emancipation Transfigured? Rethinking Mental Slavery, Racialism, and Bob Marley's Legacy," *JahWorks,* February 6, 2005.

Suede, Michael. "What Percentage of the US Adult Population Has a Felony Conviction?," *Libertarian News,* June 5, 2014, https://www.libertariannews.org/2014/06/05/what-percentage-of-us-adult-population-that-has-a-felony-conviction/.

Tafari, Ras Sekou S. In the introduction to *The Wise Mind of H.I.M. Emperor Haile Sellassie* by H.I.H. Prince Ermias Sahle Selassie, Frontline Books, 2004.

Tani, E. and Kaé Sera. *False Nationalism, False Internationalism: Class Contradictions in the Armed Struggle,* A Seeds Beneath the Snow Publication, 1985.

TePaske, John J. *Three American Empires,* Harper & Row, 1967.

Turner, Terisa E. *Arise Ye Mighty People!: Gender, Class and Race in Popular Struggles,* Africa World Press, 1994.

Van Sertima, Ivan. *Early America Revisited,* Transaction Publishers, 1998.

Wade, Lizzie. "Traces of Some of South America's Earliest People Found Under Ancient Dirt Pyramid," *Science,* May 24, 2017, http://www.sciencemag.org/news/2017/05/traces-some-south-america-s-earliest-people-found-under-ancient-dirt-pyramid.

Wiener, Alter. *From a Name to a Number: A Holocaust Survivor's Autobiography,* AuthorHouse, 2007.

Wilson, Woodrow. *The New Freedom: A Call for the Emancipation of the Generous Energies of a People,* Doubleday, Page & Company, 1913.

Windsor, Rudolph R. *From Babylon to Timbuktu,* Windsor Golden Series, 1969.

Worrell, Rodney. *Pan-Africanism in Barbados: An Analysis of the Activities of the Major 20th-Century Pan-African Formations in Barbados*, New Academia Publishing, 2005.

Zinn, Howard. *A People's History of the United States (Abridged Teaching Edition)*, The New Press, 2003.

Zirin, Dave. "Why Arnold Killed Tookie," *AlterNet*, December 13, 2005, https://www.alternet.org/story/29497/why_arnold_killed_tookie.

Acknowledgments

This book could not have been completed without help from the following people: Ras Miles Jacob Marley, founder of the Rastafari UniverSoul Fellowship, saved a copy of an early draft of this book when my computer crashed. Orus Barker, a spiritual brother and religious scholar, helped by challenging me on the content of the final draft. David Ensminger edited a draft before Akashic got their hands on it. Rah Amen played on many of the songs I wrote and has kept a bright light in his heart through some very tough times. Ras Michael, Ras Sela Judah Fari, Empress Iffiya Seales, Binghi Irie Lion, Jah B, Maxine Stowe, Haile Israel, Christopher Liontree, Aslon Walkon, Al Bailey, Isa Azuriah, Tftka Dawidalle, Jake Homiak, and Ras Alan all helped personify the Rastafari movement in my life. Ramona Africa and Lorenzo Ervin first brought revolutionary social action down to earth for me and my cohorts in the early nineties. Ian MacKaye, Mark Andersen, and Tim Kerr have remained an embodiment of DIY integrity and strategy in a sick capitalist paradigm. Chuck Marsh, the great permaculturist, brought me to Jamaica at just the right time. Johnny Temple believed in me enough to whip this work into shape. Brady Brickner-Wood did some invaluable editorial work on this book as well. Stephen Smith continues to inspire me to no end, and the mother of my children, Arlaya Swan, allowed me the time to focus on all this while working so hard for our family and tirelessly pointing the way forward.

THE HALF THAT'S NEVER BEEN TOLD
by Doctor Dread
272 pages, trade paperback original, $16.95

"Doctor Dread may just prove to be as gripping a storyteller as he was a record producer. In this revelatory vignette-filled offering, he bends the rules with an unorthodox literary style, unveiling a torrent of chronicles that are spontaneous, colorful, richly authentic and brazen. This is a unique work on many levels. Doctor Dread does offer new and intimate insights into the legends of Jamaican culture. . . . Highly recommended." —*Jamaica Gleaner*

"A gem . . . Real music heads will truly enjoy this book. . . . For anyone who is a fan of Reggae music, this book is a must-have."
—*Baltimore Times*

JONAH SEES GHOSTS
by Mark J. Sullivan, III
190 pages, trade paperback original, $13.95

"Written with insight and compassion, this is a stunning look at the addictive personality of an adolescent boy in an alcoholic family." —*Library Journal*, starred review

"Mark Sullivan writes with beautiful, introspective clarity. In young Jonah, he captures perfectly the conviction of perception that only the young have." —Henry Rollins

"Jonah, with the heart of a transcendentalist, travels out of body in a spirit world full of meanies and walking corpses and brings a report of redemption back to the land of the living. . . . Sullivan leaves us wiser in our admiration for his remarkable first novel."
—John Rolfe Gardiner, author of *Great Dream from Heaven*

LOVE MAPS
by Eliza Factor
240 pages, trade paperback original, $15.95

"Powerfully written . . . . Factor reveals this arresting tale through solid character development and a well-paced narrative. From its tense opening chapter to its memorable conclusion, this is a read-in-one-sitting trip." —*Publishers Weekly*

"Compelling . . . a poignant picture of familial and romantic love and their complexities." —*Library Journal*

"Memorable and touching . . . a commendable achievement that captures the interrelation of fear and love in the unbalanced reality of modern adulthood." —*San Francisco Book Review*

WE ARE THE CLASH
by Mark Andersen and Ralph Heibutzki
376 pages, trade paperback original, $18.95

"The Clash's final chapter, after guitarist Mick Jones' 1983 depar-
ture, has largely been forgotten—until this book, in which authors
Mark Andersen and Ralph Heibutzki argue that the punk pioneers
were still creating vital music to the very end."
—*Rolling Stone*, One of RS Picks/New Books for Summer 2018

"At long last, The Clash's final incarnation has been definitively
chornicled . . . I was riveted, unable to put it down."
—The Baker, from the foreword

SPOKE: IMAGES AND STORIES FROM THE 1980S WASHINGTON, DC PUNK SCENE
compiled by Scott Crawford
128 pages, hardcover, $24.95

FEATURING: Bad Brains, The Teen Idles, Black Market Baby, Soa,
Minor Threat, Government Issue, Void, Iron Cross, The Faith,
Scream, Marginal Man, Gray Matter, Beefeater, King Face, Rites
of Spring, Dag Nasty, Embrace, Soulside, Fire Party, Shudder To
Think, Ignition, Fugazi, Swiz, The Nation of Ulysses, and Jawbox.

"The pictures, which include some posed portraits but are mostly concert shots, are the chief attraction. They freeze moments of adolescent
release, vein-bulging intensity and sweaty communion that fuses
performer and audience . . . Vivid and evocative." —*Washington Post*

DANCE OF DAYS: UPDATED EDITION
by Mark Andersen and Mark Jenkins
460 pages, trade paperback original, $23.95

"A truly compelling narrative . . . a powerful piece of cultural
reporting." —*Washington Post*

"For anyone interested in the power of independent music, this is
an overdue insight into a vibrant, homegrown scene." —*Mojo*